Introducing

ENGLISH GRAMMAR

Geoffrey Leech

PENGUIN ENGLISH

PENGUIN ENGLISH

Published by the Penguin Group
Penguin Books Ltd, 27 Wrights Lane, London W8 5TZ, England
Penguin Books USA Inc., 375 Hudson Street, New York, New York 10014, USA
Penguin Books Australia Ltd, Ringwood, Victoria, Australia
Penguin Books Canada Ltd, 10 Alcorn Avenue, Toronto, Ontario, Canada M4V 3B2
Penguin Books (NZ) Ltd, 182–190 Wairau Road, Auckland 10, New Zealand

Penguin Books Ltd, Registered Offices: Harmondsworth, Middlesex, England

First published 1992
1 3 5 7 9 10 8 6 4 2

Text copyright © Geoffrey Leech, 1992
All rights reserved

The moral right of the author has been asserted

Set in 10/13½ pt Lasercomp Times Roman
Printed in England by Clays Ltd, St Ives plc

Introduction to the series

The aim of this series is to meet a need which has often been expressed by students encountering linguistics for the first time – to have a brief, clear and convenient guide to central concepts in the various branches of the subject, which would help them develop painlessly a sense of its range and depth. The idea is to provide a comprehensive outline of an area, which can be used as a general backup for lectures, a supplementary index for textbooks, and an opportune aid for revision. The information is organized alphabetically, for convenience of look-up, but it is presented discursively, with copious cross-references. The result is a somewhat unconventional kind of reference book – half-dictionary, half-encyclopaedia – but one which offers considerable gains in accessibility and comprehension. The order of headings is based on word-by-word alphabetization.

We have chosen topics for the first books in the series which are widely taught in introductory undergraduate and postgraduate courses. Along with linguistics itself, we have dealt with phonetics, English grammar, sociolinguistics, and psycholinguistics. Each has been written by an acknowledged leader in the field, in consultation with the general editor, and the result is a series which I believe conveys with authority, clarity, currency and consistency the core elements of this fascinating subject.

David Crystal

A **bold typeface** within an entry indicates a cross-reference to another entry. Major cross-references are usually at the end of an entry.

A semi-bold typeface indicates an extension or subdivision of a head-word.

Bold italics indicate emphasis without cross-reference.

Bold italics also indicate a reference to a verb, where the different verb forms are irrelevant. (E.g., *look* refers to *look/ looks/looked/looking*.)

~   A swing dash indicates a relation between alternative forms of the same basic word or pattern, e.g. *boy* ~ *boys*.

( )   Round brackets in examples indicate something which is optional, i.e., can be omitted or ignored.

[ ]   Square brackets are sometimes used for clarity in examples to indicate the boundaries of a major constituent, especially a clause.

| Vertical lines in examples are sometimes used to separate main elements of a clause, e.g., subject, verb phrase, and object.

*   An asterisk indicates an unacceptable sequence of words.

NOTE   The terminology in this book is closely based on that of Randolph Quirk et al.: *A Comprehensive Grammar of the English Language.*

(6)

abstract noun A **noun** which denotes an abstraction, i.e. which does not refer to anything physical or concrete. Common types of abstract noun are (a) nouns denoting events, actions or states, such as *arrival, invitation, hope*; (b) nouns denoting qualities, such as *happiness, size, absurdity*; (c) nouns denoting mental or perceptual phenomena, such as *idea, music, vision*. Abstract nouns contrast with concrete nouns, such as *window, student* and *steam*, which denote physically identifiable entities or substances. Like concrete nouns, abstract nouns can be **count**, **non-count**, or both. For example, *arrival* is count (as the plural form *arrivals* shows), *happiness* is non-count (as the non-occurrence of **happinesses* shows), and *vision* can be both: *We need vision* and *We need visions* are both possible, but with a difference of meaning.

Many abstract nouns are derived from **verbs** (e.g., *arrive* ~ *arrival, invite* ~ *invitation*), or derived from **adjectives** (e.g., *happy* ~ *happiness, wide* ~ *width*). Such derived nouns are typically recognizable by their suffixes (e.g., *-ation, -ion, -ness, -ity, -ance, -ence, -hood, -ing, -al*). Some, however, are identical in form to a corresponding verb (e.g., *hope, love, release, mention*).

accusative case A more traditional term for **objective case**.

active, active voice The term applied to a verb phrase which is not passive. (See **passive**; **voice**.)

actor   see **agent** (2)

adjectival clause   A term sometimes used for a **clause** which, like an **adjective**, modifies a **noun**, e.g., a **relative clause**. Compare: *an expensive present* (where *expensive* is an adjective) with *a present which cost a great deal* (where *which cost a great deal* is a relative clause).

adjective   A large class of words (e.g., *good, bad, new, accurate, careful*) which define more precisely the reference of a **noun** or **pronoun**. A typical adjective can occur before a noun, as in *a good plan, this bad weather, our new manager, accurate predictions*. (In this position, the adjective is said to premodify the **head** of a **noun phrase**.) A typical adjective can also occur after the verb *be*, as in *The plan was good; The weather is bad; Your predictions were accurate*. (In this position, the adjective is said to be the **complement**, or subject complement.) Most common adjectives can be preceded by **degree adverbs** such as *very* (e.g., *very good, very accurate*) and can also be used in a **comparative** form such as *better, older, more accurate*, or in a **superlative** form such as *best, oldest, most accurate*. Many of these gradable adjectives form their comparative and superlative forms with the *-er* and *-est* suffixes, e.g., *cold ~ colder ~ coldest*. Whereas the above statements define 'typical' adjectives, many adjectives fail to match one or more of these criteria: *asleep* cannot be used in front of a noun, and *sole* (as in *the sole survivor*) cannot be used after the verb *be*. Most common adjectives form pairs which contrast in terms of meaning: *good ~ bad, wide ~ narrow; useful ~ useless*, etc. Many adjectives are derived from other words (especially nouns), and are easy to recognize by their suffixes. Some of the most common adjective suffixes are: *-al* (as in *equal*), *-ous* (as in *famous*), *-ic* (as in *basic*), *-y* (as in *sleepy*), *-ful* (as in *beautiful*) and *-less* (as in *hopeless*).

adjective phrase   A phrase in which an **adjective** is the **head**, or main word. The simplest kind of adjective phrase is one which consists simply of an adjective, as in *The meeting was noisy*. An adjective phrase can be made more complex by adding **modifiers** (especially **degree adverbs**) before the adjective: *The meeting was very/too noisy*. Also, the adjective can be followed by other words which modify or complement the meaning of the adjective: *too poor to feed themselves*; *too early for breakfast*; *useful enough*; *funnier than the last show*, etc. An adjective phrase can contain a **comparative clause**, as in *The weather this winter has been colder than I can remember*. In terms of their function, adjective phrases generally act as **complements**: either as subject complement, as in *The meeting was too long*, or as **object complement**, as in *I found the meeting too long*.

adjunct   An element which is part of a **clause** or **sentence**, in which it modifies the verb (or the verb plus other elements). Adjunct is another term for **adverbial**, but its use is often limited to adverbials which are closely integrated with the rest of the clause, e.g., adverbials of **time**, of **place**, of **manner**, of instrument, etc., as in *They then attacked me*; *They attacked me in the street*; *They attacked me fiercely*; *They attacked me with knives*, etc. Adjuncts are generally optional parts of the sentence, but in certain cases adjuncts cannot be omitted, e.g., the adjunct of place in *She put the book on the shelf*. Compare **linking adverbial**; **sentence adverbial**.

adverb A major class of words, primarily consisting of words which modify **verbs, adjectives**, and other adverbs, e.g., adverbs of **time** (*now, then*, etc.), of **place** (*there, somewhere*, etc.), of **manner** (*well, carefully*, etc.), of **degree** (*so, very*, etc.), and a wide range of other words which do not fit into such easily defined categories: *just, either, however, actually*, etc. Adverbs form a disparate set of words; in fact, some grammarians have doubted the viability of the adverb class. There is a fairly major distinction, for example, between words capable of taking an **adverbial** function in the clause (e.g., *then, there, quickly, much*), and degree words capable of premodifying other words such as adjectives, adverbs, and determiners (e.g., *very* in *very large, very quickly*, and *very many*). However, these sub-classes overlap considerably. Another way of dividing the class of adverbs into distinct categories is to separate a closed class of **function words** (*now, where, so, too, just*, etc.) and an open class of derived words, chiefly adverbs in *-ly* (e.g., *quickly, saliently, refreshingly*). Some adverbs (e.g., *long, early, later*) are identical in form to adjectives to which they are also closely related in meaning. (See **adverbial; modifier**.)

adverb phrase A **phrase** in which an **adverb** is the main word, or **head**. An adverb phrase may consist of one word (an adverb alone), as in *She hits the ball **hard***, or of two words, as in *She hits the ball **extremely hard*** (where *hard* is modified by another adverb, *extremely*), or of a longer sequence of words, as in *She hits the ball **hard enough to defeat the skill of many more experienced opponents***. (See **adverb**.)

adverbial An element of a **clause** or **sentence** which adds extra meaning about the event or state of affairs described. Adverbials are the most peripheral of the clause elements **subject** (S), **verb phrase** (V), **object** (O), **complement** (C) and **adverbial** (A) which make up the structure of a clause. Adverbials are normally optional. That is, they can be omitted without changing the relations of meaning and structure in the rest of the clause: *suddenly* is optional in *She left suddenly* (compare *She left*). They are also typically mobile – i.e. can occur in more than one position in the clause, as in *She left suddenly* ~ *She suddenly left* ~ *Suddenly she left*. A further point about adverbials is that more than one of them can occur in the same clause: *At midnight, she secretly left to meet Heathcliff.* Adverbials belong to varied meaning categories, e.g., adverbials of **time**-*when*, of **duration**, of **frequency**, of **place**, of **manner**, of means, of instrument, of **degree**, of **purpose**. In many cases, these categories can be distinguished as answering different question words (*when, where, how, why*) or question phrases (*how long, how often, how much, how far*):

> *When did she leave? At midnight.*
> *How did she leave? Secretly.*
> *Why did she leave? To meet Heathcliff.*

In spite of their name, adverbials do not necessarily contain adverbs: they may consist of an **adverb phrase**, as in *She left* (*very*) *suddenly*, but they may also consist of a **prepositional phrase** (*at midnight, through the window*), or of a **noun phrase** (*last night, the week before last*), or of an **adverbial clause** (*as soon as she could*).

adverbial clause   A **clause** which acts as an **adverbial** in the **main clause** or **sentence** it belongs to. Adverbial clauses can be said to modify the rest of the main clause – i.e. they add extra information in terms of time, condition, concession, cause or reason, result, etc. In *She suddenly left **when the police entered the building***, the adverbial clause *when the police entered the building* tells us more about the circumstances in which she left: it is an adverbial of time, answering the question *When did she leave?* While acting as an adverbial in the main clause, the adverbial clause also contains its own clause elements: *the police* (**subject**), *entered* (**verb phrase**), and *the building* (**object**). In addition, most adverbial clauses begin with a **conjunction**, signalling their link with the **main clause**. Examples of such conjunctions are *when*, *since*, *before*, *after*, *until*, *as*, *while* (conjunctions of time); *if*, *unless* (conditional conjunctions); *although*, *though* (concessive conjunctions); *because*, *as*, *since* (conjunctions of cause or reason). Like other adverbials, adverbial clauses are typically mobile, and can occur either before or after the other elements of the main clause. Compare:

> *You should lie down [if you feel ill].*
> *[If you feel ill], you should lie down.*

Adverbial clauses are varied in structure as well as in meaning. For example, there are different kinds of non-finite adverbial clause:

> *I opened the window [to let in some fresh air].*
> *[Smiling sweetly], she greeted her uncles.*
> *He died [forgotten by all but his closest friends].*

(See **adverbial; subordinate clause.**)

agent (1) A **noun phrase** (or sometimes, a **noun clause**) following *by* in a **passive** construction, and corresponding to the **subject** of an **active** clause: in *Several children were rescued by the police*, *the police* is the agent. Compare *the police* as the subject of an active clause: *The police rescued several children.* An agent typically refers to the 'doer' of an action signalled by the verb (see (2) below). But in some passive constructions, the agent is not a 'doer', i.e. does not identify the performer of an action: in *The crime was seen on television by millions of people*, the agent refers to passive spectators. The agent of a passive verb is frequently omitted: *Several children were rescued; The mystery has been solved.* (See **passive voice**.) (2) Agent is also used more broadly to indicate the 'doer' of an action, as contrasted with the 'doee' – the person, thing, etc. to which something happens. Thus, nouns such as *employer*, *teacher* and *manager*, referring to the 'doer' of a certain task or role, are often called 'agent nouns'.

agreement   Another term for **concord**.

alternative conditional clause   An **adverbial clause** which conveys the idea that the happening described in the main clause depends on two alternative conditions: *Whether you love him or not, he deserves your respect*; *It will be a close match, whether she beats me or I beat her.* Alternative conditions are expressed by *whether . . . or . . .* (See **conditional clause**.)

alternative question   A question in which the speaker offers the hearer a closed choice between two or more alternative possibilities: *Is the child male or female?*; *Would you like orange juice, grapefruit juice, or tomato juice?* The word *or* signals the relation between the alternatives. Unlike *yes–no* **questions**, alternative questions normally end with a falling intonation contour. There are also reported alternative questions: these are subordinate **nominal clauses** in which the alternatives are expressed by *whether . . . or . . .* (Compare **alternative conditional clause**.) *Whether* can generally be replaced by *if*: *They asked her **whether/if** the child was male or female*. (See **question**; **reported speech**.)

antecedent   An expression to which a **pronoun** refers (or – more properly – co-refers), and which normally precedes the pronoun in the text. The term is used primarily for the noun or nominal expression which precedes a **relative pronoun** such as *who* or *which*. For example, in *the girl who had a heart transplant, (the) girl* is the antecedent of *who*. Sometimes the antecedent is a whole clause or sentence: *Jeremy has no brothers or sisters, which is a pity*. (Here the antecedent of *which* is *Jeremy has no brothers or sisters*.) By extension, the term antecedent also applies to an expression to which a personal pronoun such as *he*, *she*, *it*, or *they* cross-refers: ***Sinbad** told the queen **he** had lost all **his** possessions*. (Here *he* and *his* refer to Sinbad, so *Sinbad* is their antecedent.) Yet another extension of the term is to apply it to an expression which follows the pronoun rather than precedes it. For example, *Marie* is the antecedent of *her* in *To **her** own family, **Marie** was just an ordinary girl*. (See **personal pronouns**; **relative clause**; **sentence relative clause**.)

***any*-words**   see **non-assertive**

apposition (adjective: **appositive**)   A relation between two constituents, such that the following statements normally apply: (a) Apposition takes place between two **noun phrases**; (b) The two constituents in apposition are in an equivalence or attribution relationship which could be expressed by the verb *be*; (c) The two constituents are juxtaposed in a single noun phrase, which can act, for example, as **subject** or **object** of a sentence.

Examples of apposition are: *George Washington, first President of the USA*; *My neighbour Mrs Randall*; *tequila, a powerful Mexican drink*. By extension, the term apposition is applied to a noun phrase juxtaposed with a co-referential **nominal clause** (e.g., *the idea/hope that the White House would change its policy* – cf. *The idea/hope was that the White House would change its policy*). An *of*-phrase in which *of* links co-referential expressions may also be termed appositive: *the city of Beirut*; *the disgrace of losing the contest*.

appositive   see **apposition**

articles   The two words *the* and *a* (*an* before vowels), known respectively as the **definite** and **indefinite articles**. They are **determiners**, beginning a **noun phrase** and typically followed by a **noun**, with or without **modifiers**: *the picture*, *a picture*; *the actor*; *an actor*; *a brilliant actor*. Normally, **proper nouns** (names) do not have a preceding article (*Paris*, *John*, etc.). Moreover, **plural** and **non-count nouns** do not have an indefinite article: *the pictures* contrasts with *pictures* in *I like the pictures* ~ *I like pictures*. Similarly, *I like the music* contrasts with *I like music*. In the case of **common nouns**, absence of *the*, signalling indefiniteness, is frequently regarded as an instance of the **zero article**. This is because it is convenient, from many points of view, to regard an initial determiner as obligatory for English noun phrases, so that the absence of an article is itself a mark of indefiniteness. (See **definite article**; **indefinite article**; **zero article**.)

aspect   The grammatical category indicating the temporal point of view from which an event, state, etc. is seen to take place. In English, two contrasts of aspect are recognized.   (a) The **progressive aspect**, e.g., *is working*, indicates that the event/state is in progress – that is, is seen from a continuing, ongoing point of view.   (b) The **perfect** (sometimes called perfective) **aspect**, e.g., *has worked*, indicates that the event/state is seen from a completed, retrospective point of view. Both aspect constructions may be combined, as in *has been working* (called perfect progressive). There are therefore four aspectual possibilities in English:

	NON-PROGRESSIVE	PROGRESSIVE
NON-PERFECT	*works*	*is working*
PERFECT	*has worked*	*has been working*

(See **perfect; progressive**.) Compare **tense**.

assertive   see **non-assertive**

asyndetic   see **asyndeton**

asyndeton (adjective: asyndetic)   The omission of connectives. This term applies more particularly to the habit of omitting *and* or *or*. Compare the normal coordination constructions

   *men, women **and** children   I love you, **and** you love me.*

with the asyndetic constructions

   men, women, children   I love you; you love me.

16

attributive adjective An **adjective** which modifies a **noun**, e.g., *a friendly neighbour, strange events*. Some adjectives (e.g., *mere, major, utter*) are attributive only: we can say *an **utter** failure*, but not **the failure was **utter***. Certain other adjectives cannot be used as attributive adjectives, e.g., we can say *The rabbit was **afraid***, but not **the **afraid** rabbit*. (See **adjective**.) Compare **predicative adjective**.

auxiliary verb A 'helping' **verb** which cannot occur without a following **main verb** (except in cases of **ellipsis**). The primary auxiliary verbs *be*, *have* and *do* are used for aspect, voice, and dummy operator functions. (These three verbs also occur as main verbs.) They are followed by non-finite forms of the verb, as in:

> *is helped* (**passive**)
> *is helping* (**progressive**)
> *has helped* (**perfect**)
> *does not complain* (dummy operator)

The other auxiliary verbs are **modal auxiliaries** (*can*, *must*, etc.), whose main function is to convey modal notions such as 'possibility', 'necessity', 'permission', and 'prediction'.

In their form, the verbs which function as auxiliaries are highly irregular:

Be has eight forms: *am, is, are, was, were, be, being, been*.
Have has four forms: *has, have, had, having*.
Do has five forms: *does, do, did, done, doing* (but *done* and *doing* are not used as auxiliary forms).
The modals have only one or two forms, e.g., *can, could*.

Auxiliary verbs can be combined, as in *may have found*, *has been taken*, **is being** *performed*. For the rules of combination, see **verb phrase**. (See **modal (auxiliary)**; **passive; perfect; progressive**.)

bare infinitive The **base form** of the verb (e.g., *be, have, take, deceive*) when used as a non-finite form, as in *I saw her **open** the safe; What we did next was **telephone** the fire service*. The most common use of the bare infinitive is following a **modal auxiliary** or the auxiliary *do*: *You should **eat** something; They didn't **see** us*. The bare infinitive contrasts with the more common **to-infinitive** (the infinitive preceded by *to*), as in *What we did next was **to telephone** the fire service*. (See **infinitive**.)

base form The uninflected form of the **verb**, i.e. the form which has no suffix, and which is also the primary form, used for representing the verb when it is put in a dictionary, e.g., *answer, eat, finish, make*. The base forms of the primary **auxiliary verbs** are *be, have*, and *do*. (See **infinitive; imperative; present tense; subjunctive**.)

block language A variety of English which has a much simplified grammar, often reduced to the use of **noun phrases** alone, without verbs, e.g., *Daily Express, No Entry, Parking for buses only, Touch-down!* Block language occurs in many different situations, but it is mainly associated with brief written public messages, such as road signs, advertising slogans, titles, headings, and headlines.

cardinal number/numeral A number such as *one, two, three, ... twenty-four, ... one hundred and sixty-five*. Cardinal numbers can be spelled out, as above, or can be written in digits, as in *1,*

2, 3, . . . 24, . . . 165, etc. Cardinal numbers are the words we use in specifying quantities, e.g., in answer to the question *How many . . .?* They are distinguished from ordinal numbers, which specify the order of items in a list: *first, second, third, fourth*, etc. (See **numerals**.)

case The variation in form of a **noun** or **pronoun** according to its role in the syntax of the sentence. Case (nominative, accusative, genitive, dative, etc.) is important in many European languages, but, historically, English has lost most of its case distinctions. The only relics of the English case system today are the **subjective** and **objective** forms of pronouns (*I, me; we, us*; etc.) and the **genitive** forms of nouns and pronouns (*boy's, my, our*, etc.), also called the **possessive** forms. Even these forms have lost some of their 'case' function in modern English (see **genitive**). (See **objective; subjective**.)

cause or reason, causative **Adverbials** of cause or reason are those expressing a link of cause and effect between two ideas, as in clauses introduced by *because, as*, or *since*: *She was angry because I was late.* **Prepositional phrases** of cause or reason are introduced by such prepositions as *because of, on account of*: *She was angry because of my late arrival.* The same basic notion can be conveyed by causative verbs such as *angered* in *My late arrival angered her.* Other examples of causative verbs are *weaken, beautify, immunize* (compare *weak, beautiful, immune*).

clause A major unit of grammar, defined formally by the elements it may contain: **subject** (S), **verb phrase** (V), **object** (O), **complement** (C) and **adverbial** (A). All five elements are illustrated in:

S	A	V	O	C
We	*always*	*found*	*the teachers*	*very helpful.*

The verb phrase is the most central and crucial element of a clause, so it is helpful to identify a clause by first identifying its **main verb**. As the above example shows, a clause can be capable of standing alone as a complete sentence. Such clauses, called **independent clauses**, are distinct from **dependent clauses**, which generally cannot stand as a complete sentence, and are marked by a signal (e.g., a **conjunction** such as *if*) showing their subordinate status. An example of a dependent clause is:

conjunction	S	V	O	A
because	*no one*	*has seen*	*Mars*	*at close quarters.*

Clauses are classified in various ways. We can classify **main clauses** on the basis of their communicative function, as **declarative, interrogative, imperative,** or **exclamatory** (see **sentence types**). We can also classify dependent, or **subordinate clauses** on the basis of their function within the main clause (as **nominal, adverbial, relative, comparative**). A third classification singles out the presence of a **finite** (or 'tensed') **verb** as crucial: on this basis, **finite clauses** are distinguished from **non-finite clauses**. For example, in contrast to *Her uncle has given her a book* (where *has* is a finite verb), the following are non-finite clauses: *having given her a book* and *to give her a book*. A further type of clause is a **verbless clause**, apparently a contradiction in terms, lacking not just the finite verb, but the whole verb phrase, for example, *Whatever the reason* in *Whatever the reason, she's less friendly than she was.* This clearly lacks the verb *be* which would be necessary to make its meaning clear: *Whatever the reason may be.* Non-finite and verbless clauses are dependent clauses, and cannot stand alone as a sentence except in unusual cases, e.g., in **block language.** (See **finite clause; independent and dependent clauses; main clause; non-finite clause; subordinate clause.**)

clause pattern   see **verb pattern**

cleft sentence   A sentence divided into two segments (hence its name 'cleft sentence') as follows:

> FIRST SEGMENT   *It + be +* **complement.**
> SECOND SEGMENT   *that/who/which/***zero** + **relative clause.**

	FIRST SEGMENT	SECOND SEGMENT
e.g. (a)	*It was my uncle*	*who gave this book to Sue.*

The most important element of a cleft sentence is the complement (following the verb *be*), which is called the 'focus'. The second segment is similar to a relative clause, and consists of a **relative pronoun** (or zero relative pronoun) followed by the rest of a clause from which the focus has been extracted. Thus, example (a) above is based on a more straightforward sentence *My uncle gave this book to Sue.* Other cleft sentences based on the same sentence would make the focus not the **subject,** but the **object** or **adverbial:**

> (b) *It was **this book** that my uncle gave to Sue.*
> (c) *It was **to Sue** that my uncle gave this book.*

The second segment of a cleft sentence is sometimes called its 'presupposition', since this part of the sentence is presented as if it were already known or presupposed to be true. Hence the cleft sentences (a)–(c), although they do not differ in basic content, 'tell the same story' in different ways, and would be appropriate to different situations.

closed word classes   see **open and closed word classes**

collective noun (or group noun)   A **noun** which refers to a group, or collection, of beings, e.g., *audience, class, committee, crowd, gang, herd, jury, party, team*. It is possible for singular collective nouns to be followed either by a singular or a plural verb form (see **number**):

> *The audience was delighted with the performance.*
> *The audience were delighted with the performance.*

Both these sentences are acceptable, although people often consider the first to be more strictly 'correct'. (See **concord**.)

command   see **imperative**

common noun   A **noun** which denotes a class of entities (people, things, etc.) or phenomena, e.g., *girl, tiger, table, mustard, pessimism*. Common nouns are distinct from **proper nouns**, which refer to an individual entity (e.g., *Delhi, Barbara, Watson*) or to a unique set of entities (e.g., [*the*] *Rockies,* [*the*] *Bahamas*). Unlike proper nouns, common nouns are normally written without an initial capital letter. The category of common nouns is very large, and includes most **count nouns** and all **non-count nouns**. Other categories largely included in that of common nouns are:

collective nouns, concrete nouns, and **abstract nouns.** All common nouns can be preceded by the **definite article** *the.* (See **noun.**)

comparative   The form of a **gradable word** which ends (according to the regular rule) in *-er,* and which indicates a comparison of two things in terms of a higher or lower position on some scale of quality or quantity, e.g., *wider, colder, happier.* There are a few irregular comparative forms, e.g., *good ~ **better**, bad ~ **worse**, little ~ **less**, many/much ~ **more**, far ~ **further**.* Regular one-syllable gradable adjectives and adverbs form their comparative by adding *-(e)r,* but for most adjectives and adverbs of more than one syllable it is necessary to add the preceding adverb *more* (or *less* for a comparison in the opposite direction), e.g., *more careful, more slowly, less natural.* The comparative forms make a series with the simple (uninflected) and superlative forms:

REGULAR *-ER*
COMPARATIVES

old	**older**	oldest
thin	**thinner**	thinnest
large	**larger**	largest
busy	**busier**	busiest
long	**longer**	longest
simple	**simpler**	simplest

OTHER COMPARATIVES

many/much	**more**	most
little	**less**	least
good	**better**	best
bad	**worse**	worst
modern	**more modern**	most modern
(etc.)		

comparative clause   A subordinate clause which modifies a **gradable word** (**adjective, adverb,** or **determiner**), and specifies the standard against which a comparison is being made:

(a) *The present mayor seems more popular [**than the last one was**].*

(b) *Nowadays the bosses have to work harder* [**than the employees work**].

(c) *It's a less valuable painting* [**than I thought**].

(d) *I drove the car as fast* [**as I could drive it with safety**].

Of these four sentences, (a)–(c) illustrate 'unequal comparison' (using the conjunction *than*), and (d) illustrates 'equal comparison' (using the conjunction *as*). Clauses of unequal comparison come after a **comparative** expression such as *older, more quickly, less popular* (see **comparative**). Clauses of equal comparison come after *as* followed by the simple form of a gradable word (e.g., *as big, as famous, as many*).

comparative phrase A **prepositional phrase** introduced by *as* or *than*, and equivalent to a **comparative clause** from which the verb has been omitted by **ellipsis**. For example, in place of (a) under **comparative clause** above, we can say simply [*than the last one*]. Here we may consider *than* to be a **preposition**, since it is followed solely by a **noun phrase**. Similarly: *Joan plays as well* [*as me*]. In **informal** English, **objective pronouns** such as *me* are used after *as* and *than*, even though they function in meaning as the subject of a verb (e.g., *play*, above). The ellipsis of the verb causes people to treat the construction *as/than* + noun phrase as equivalent to a prepositional phrase.

comparison see **comparative; comparative clause**

complement The element of a **clause** which typically follows the verb *be*, and which consists either of an **adjective (phrase)** or a **noun phrase**: *Everyone was **happy**; The party has been **extremely enjoyable**; William is **the new manager***. Other **linking verbs** may substitute for *be* here: *Everyone **was feeling** tired; William **became***

the new manager. This type of complement is called a **subject complement**, because it describes what the **subject** refers to (*William*, etc.). Other complements are called **object complements**, because they follow the **object**, and describe what the object refers to: *We found everyone **happy**; They have appointed William **the new manager**.* (See **object complement**.)

complementation of verbs   see **verb pattern**

complex conjunction/preposition   A **conjunction** or **preposition** consisting of more than one (written) word, e.g. *in order that, so long as, instead of, up to, with reference to.*

complex prepositions   see **preposition**

complex sentence   A sentence which has one or more **subordinate clauses**. Compare **compound sentence**.

compound   A word which contains two or more other words, e.g., *goldfish* (consisting of *gold + fish*), *left-handed* (consisting of *left + hand + -ed*), and *gas cooker* (consisting of *gas + cooker*). We cannot rely on punctuation (e.g., the use of a hyphen) to identify a compound. What makes a compound a compound is rather the ability of its parts to 'stick together' as a single word for purposes of grammatical behaviour and meaning. In English, there is, in particular, a tendency for two nouns to combine together into a single compound noun (e.g., *airport, security officer*). Moreover, there is a further tendency for these compounds to combine with other nouns or compounds into still larger combinations, e.g., *airport security officer.*

compound sentence   A **sentence** which contains two or more **clauses** linked by **coordination** e.g., *We went to meet her at the airport, **but** the plane was delayed.* Compare **complex sentence**.

concessive adverbial, concessive clause   An adverbial clause or other adverbial which expresses a contrast of meaning or implication of 'concession' in relation to the clause of which it is part. Concessive clauses are introduced by such **conjunctions** as *although* and *though*: [***Although the car was badly damaged***], *none of the passengers was hurt*. Concessive **phrases** are introduced by such **prepositions** as *despite* and *in spite of*: *We enjoyed our holiday* [***in spite of the weather***]. (See **adverbial; adverbial clause**.)

concessive conjunctions   see **adverbial clause**

concord (also called **agreement**)   In the most general terms, concord is a relation between two elements, such that they match one another in terms of some grammatical feature. In English, the most important type of concord is '**number** concord' between **subject** and (**finite**) **verb**. This means that a singular subject is followed by a singular verb (e.g., *My brother works in the city*), and a plural subject is followed by a plural verb (e.g., *My brothers work in the city*). A breach of concord (as in **My brother work in the city*) is ungrammatical in standard English. However, there are frequent exceptions to this general rule, and explanations of many of them make use of the concept of **notional concord** – the idea that the subject and verb are supposed to agree in terms of meaning, rather than strictly in terms of form. For example, the use of a **plural** verb after a **collective noun** such as *crowd* or after the **indefinite pronoun** *none* can be explained if we consider that the subject in (a) and (b) implies the involvement of more than one person:

(a) *The jury have come to their decision.*

(b) *None of our family take sugar in their tea.*

In addition to subject–verb concord, there is also noun–pronoun concord, i.e. agreement between a pronoun and its **antecedent** in terms of **number, person,** and **gender** (e.g., *Mary . . . she . . .; James . . . he . . .; the house . . . it . . .*). This, again, is influenced by 'notional concord', as we see from the use of the plural *their* in (a) and (b) above.

concrete noun   A noun having reference to physical phenomena, whether persons, animals, things, or substances, e.g., *student, rabbit, bus, grease.* Contrast with **abstract noun**.

conditional clause   An **adverbial clause** expressing a condition. Most conditional clauses begin with the conjunction *if* (*if*-clauses). Another conditional conjunction, with negative meaning, is *unless*. Rarer conditional conjunctions are *so long as, as long as, provided that,* and *on condition that*:

(a) [*If you take this medicine*], *you will feel better.*

(b) *Emotions are dangerous* [*unless they are controlled*].

(c) *You can stay here* [*provided that you look after yourselves*].

When their verb is in the **hypothetical past** tense, conditional clauses express 'unreal' meaning:

(d) [*If she **knew** about his behaviour*], *she would never forgive him.*

(e) *I would have invited you* [*if I **had** realized you were in town*].

Sentence (e) illustrates the hypothetical **past perfect**, referring to an unreal, or imaginary, happening in the past. (See **hypothetical past; subjunctive**.)

conditional conjunctions   see **adverbial clause**

conditional tense   A term sometimes used for the **hypothetical past** or the *were*-subjunctive.

conjunct (1) Another term for **linking adverbial** (e.g., *however*, *therefore, moreover*). (2) One of the constituents of a coordinate construction. For example, in the coordinate **noun phrase** *John Smith and his parents, John Smith* and *his parents* are two conjuncts, linked by *and*.

conjunction   A term which refers generally to words which have a conjoining or linking role in grammar. In practice, 'conjunction' denotes two rather different classes of words: coordinating conjunctions (*and, or, but*, etc.) and subordinating conjunctions (*if, when, because*, etc.). These are sometimes called 'coordinators' and 'subordinators' respectively. The coordinators are used to coordinate, or link, two or more units of the same status (e.g., two main clauses, or two noun phrases). The subordinators, on the other hand, are placed at the beginning of a subordinate clause, to link it into the main clause. (See **coordination; subordinate clause; subordination**.)

conjunctions of cause or reason   see **adverbial clause**

construction   A term used generally to signify a grammatical way of combining constituents into larger constituents. For example, the '**progressive** construction' combines a form of the verb *be* with the *-ing* form of a second verb.

continuous   see **progressive**

contracted form, contraction   A reduced or shortened form of a word. For example, the negative word *not* is frequently contracted to *n't* in speech (e.g., *isn't, wasn't, couldn't*). The auxiliary verbs *be*, *have*, *will* and *would*, and the main verb *be*, are frequently contracted (when they are **operators**) as follows:

CONTRACTIONS OF *BE*:   *am ~ 'm   is ~ 's   are ~ 're*
CONTRACTIONS OF *HAVE*:   *have ~ 've   has ~ 's   had ~ 'd*
CONTRACTION OF *WILL*:   *will ~ 'll*
CONTRACTION OF *WOULD*:   *would ~ 'd*
e.g.   *I'm, she's, they're, we've, John's, you'd, it'll.*

contrast, clause of   see **concessive clause**

coordinate clause   see **compound sentence; coordination**

coordinating conjunction, coordinator   see **conjunction**

coordination   The joining of two or more constituents of equivalent status, normally by the use of a coordinating **conjunction**, so as to form a larger grammatical unit having the same function as its parts would have on their own. For example, in

(a)   *Do you know* [₁[₂ *Mr Smith* ₂] *and* [₃ *his family* ₃]₁]?

the two noun phrases *Mr Smith* and *his family* are coordinated in order to form a larger, coordinate noun phrase *Mr Smith and his family*. Thus all three of the constituents (1, 2 and 3) are of the same basic kind. Coordination can take place at different levels of syntax: (a) shows coordination between phrases; (b) shows coordination between clauses; and (c) shows coordination between words:

  (b) [[*These photographs are yours*], but [*those are mine*]].
  (c) *The children who come* [[*first*], [*second*] or [*third*]] *will each win a prize.*

These examples illustrate the basic pattern of coordination, but there are many variations of this pattern (see particularly **asyndeton; correlative**). Compare **subordination**.

copula   The term given to the verb *be*, and sometimes to other **linking verbs**, when used as a main verb.

copular verb, copulative verb   Terms sometimes applied to **linking verbs**, i.e. the verb *be* and verbs which resemble the verb *be* in their connecting function. Examples of such verbs are *become* and *remain*.

correlative   A term used of a construction in which two parts of a sentence are linked together by two words – one word belonging to one part, and the other word belonging to the other. An instance of correlative **coordination** is: *The battle took place* [*both on the sea **and** on land*]. Two prepositional phrases are here conjoined by placing *both* in front of one constituent and *and* in front of the other. The use of correlative words adds emphasis and clarity to the construction. Other correlative coordinators are *either . . . or . . .* , *neither . . . nor . . .* , and *not only . . . but . . .* **Subordination**, as well as coordination, can be correlative: *If the car is too old for repair, then it will have to be scrapped.* Here the adverb *then* in the main clause reinforces the conditional meaning of *if* in the subordinate clause (see **conditional clause**).

count noun (also called **countable noun**)   A **noun** which has both a singular and a plural form (e.g., *picture ~ pictures, child ~ children, attack ~ attacks*). Count nouns can also be preceded by the **indefinite article** *a/an* (e.g., *a child, an attack*) or, in the plural, by words such as *many, few, these,* or the cardinal numbers *2, 3, 4, . . .* (e.g., *many pictures, these children, three attacks*). (Note that words like *sheep* and *deer*, which are unchanged in the plural, are nevertheless count nouns, because they combine with such 'counting words' as in *many/three/these sheep.*) Count nouns contrast with **non-count nouns**, which do not have a plural, and do not combine with these 'counting words', e.g., *blood, silver, money, furniture, information, advice.* Many nouns, however, can be either count or non-count, depending on their meaning and context. For example, *glass* is non-count when referring to the transparent substance, but count when referring to glass vessels or spectacles: *How much glass do you need?* (i.e. 'to glaze these windows') contrasts with *How many glasses do you need?* (i.e. for drinks, at a party). Many words which are principally count nouns can exceptionally be used as non-count nouns, and vice versa (e.g., *food* is generally non-count, but when talking of baby foods or pet foods, we use it as a count noun). (See **non-count noun; noun; plural**.)

declarative clause see **clause**

defining relative clause Another name for **restrictive relative clauses**. (See **restrictive and non-restrictive relative clauses**.)

definite article The word *the*, the most common word in English. *The* is a **determiner**, and normally introduces a **noun phrase**. Its function is to indicate that the noun phrase refers to something which is uniquely identifiable in the shared knowledge of the speaker and hearer. For example, by saying *on the ship*, a speaker implies that hearers can work out *which* ship is meant. Contrast with the use of the **indefinite article** (e.g., *a ship*). (See **articles; generic**.)

degree adverb/adverbial An **adverb(ial)** which indicates the degree or extent to which some quality or quantity applies to the situation described, e.g., *very quickly*; *utterly useless*; *He loves her to distraction*. Degree adverb(ial)s normally modify **gradable words**, especially gradable **adjectives**, **adverbs** and **verbs**. (See **adverb; adverbial; gradable word**.)

deictic (abstract noun: **deixis**) /'daɪktɪk, 'daɪksɪs/ A word which points to, or indicates, what it refers to. Common deictic words are the **demonstratives** *this*, *that*, *these* and *those*; the place adverbs *here* and *there*; and the time adverbs *now* and *then*. Deictics shift their reference according to the context in which they are uttered. For example, the meaning of *I'll meet you **there this** evening* is not clear, unless we know from the context (either from what has been said, or from the situation outside language) which place is meant by *there*, and which evening is meant by *this* *evening.* 'Deixis' is the noun corresponding to the adjective deictic.

demonstrative   The four words *this, that, these* and *those.* When they are followed by some other word (especially a noun) in a **noun phrase,** they are demonstrative **determiners:** *this machine; that old bicycle; these people; those pictures we saw last week.* When they act as the **head** (and typically the only word) of a noun phrase, they are demonstrative pronouns: *This is a fascinating programme; Whose gloves are those?* The demonstratives are so called because they have the function of 'showing' or 'pointing to' something in the context. They are **deictic** words. Of the four demonstratives, *this* and *that* are singular, while *these* and *those* are plural. *This* and *these* have 'immediate' or 'nearby' reference, while *that* and *those* have 'non-immediate' or 'distant' reference. (Note that *that* is not always a demonstrative: it can also be a **conjunction** or a **relative pronoun.**) (See *that*-**clause.**)

demonstrative pronouns   see **demonstrative; pronouns**

dependent clause   A **clause** which is dependent on (i.e. included in the structure of) another clause. (See **independent and dependent clauses.** See also the similar concept of **subordinate clause.**)

derivational morphology   see **morphology**

determiner   A word which 'determines' or 'specifies' how the reference of a **noun phrase** is to be understood. For example, *this* determines the reference of *table* in *this table:* it tells us which or what table is intended. Determiners normally precede a **noun,**

and indeed precede all other words in a noun phrase: *this old table you bought*; *some other people*; *what a strange sight*. The **articles** *the* and *a/an* are the most common determiners. Other determiners are the **demonstrative** determiners *this*, *that*, *these* and *those*; **possessive** determiners (or pronouns) *my*, *you*, *their*, etc.; **indefinite determiners** such as *all*, *some*, *much*, *each*; *wh*-determiners such as *which*, *what* and *whose*. In position, some determiners can precede others: *all* (known as a predeterminer) precedes *the* in *all the dishes*; *the* precedes *many* (known as a postdeterminer) in *the many meetings I have attended*. Words like *the*, *this*, and *my* are known as central determiners. The determiners are an example of a closed class of function words. (See **function words**; **word-class**.)

direct object   An **object** which follows the **verb phrase** and which typically indicates the person, thing, etc. directly affected by the main verb's meaning: in *Many animals rear their young in burrows*, *their young* is the object. Direct objects are contrasted with **indirect objects**: in *I've sent Maggie a thank-you letter*, *Maggie* is the indirect object, and a *thank-you letter* is the direct object. (For further details, see **object**.)

direct question   see **question**

direct speech   A mode of reporting what someone has said, in which we reproduce the actual words spoken or written. In narrative, direct speech is normally signalled by being enclosed in quotation marks: in *'Look after yourself,' said Jonah*, *Look after yourself* is in direct speech. Direct speech contrasts with indirect, or reported speech: *Jonah told me to look after myself*. (See **reported speech**.)

discontinuous phrase A **phrase** divided into two (or more) segments which are separated by words not part of the phrase. For example, in *A time will come when the world will regret this decision*, the predicate *will come* separates the first part of the subject noun phrase (*A time*...) from the rest (...*when the world*...). The discontinuity could be avoided if *will come* were moved to the end of the sentence: *A time when* ... *decision will come*. However, discontinuity is sometimes desirable, as it avoids an unbalanced sentence. (See **end-weight**.)

disjunct see **sentence adverbial**

dummy operator see **auxiliary verb**; **dummy word**; **negation**; **operator**; **past simple**

dummy subject see **dummy word**; **existential** *there*

dummy, dummy word A word which fills a grammatical position, but is 'empty' of meaning. For example, the verb *do*, used as an auxiliary, is often called the **dummy operator**, because it has no meaning of its own, but exists simply to fill the 'slot' of **operator**, when an operator is needed to form (e.g.) negative or interrogative sentences. In a similar way, *it* can be called a **dummy subject** when it fills the subject slot in sentences like: *It's a pity that they wasted so much time*. Compare with *That they wasted so much time is a pity*. (See **extraposition**; **introductory** *it*; **operator**.)

duration adverb/adverbial An **adverb(ial)** specifying length of time e.g., *The hostages have not been seen **for several years***; *I waited **all night** for a phone call*. (See **adverb**; **adverbial**.)

echo question   A question which echoes a previous utterance, and amounts to a request for the repetition of that utterance (or at least of part of it). We use echo questions either because we do not fully hear or understand what was said, or because its content is too surprising to be believed. For example:

> (*It cost $5000.*)   *HOW much did it cost?*
> (*His son's an osteopath.*)   *His son's a WHAT?*

Such questions are usually spoken with a rising intonation, and with a strong emphasis on the **wh-word** (*what*, *who*, *how*, etc.). (See **question** ; **wh-question**.)

-ed clause (also called a **past participle construction**)   A subordinate **non-finite clause** in which the **main verb** (and only verb word) is an **-ed form**. For example:

> (a) *a letter written by Jane Austen.*
> (b) *Refused entry to the country, we had to return home.*

Some -*ed* clauses, like (a), modify nouns, and are therefore adjectival, similar to **relative clauses**. Other -*ed* clauses, like (b), are **adverbial**. Generally speaking, an -*ed* clause is passive in meaning, but lacks a subject. (The implied subject is the **head** of the **noun phrase**, as in (a), or the **subject** of the **main clause**, as in (b).) But sometimes an adverbial -*ed* clause does have a subject, e.g., *All things considered, the meeting was a success.* (See **-ed form; non-finite clause**.)

-ed form, -ed participle   The past participle form of a **verb**, used to form the **perfect** after *have* (e.g., *has changed*); to form the **passive** after *be* (e.g., *are changed*); and to form the verb in a non-finite *-ed* **clause** (e.g., ***Convinced*** *of his innocence, the Queen ordered his release*). The *-ed* form of regular verbs ends in *-ed* (e.g., *looked, prepared, tied*). The *-ed* form of **irregular verbs** takes many different forms (e.g., *blown, sung, sent*), some ending in *-en* (e.g., *been, taken, eaten*). With regular verbs and many irregular verbs, the *-ed* participle is identical to the **past tense** form.

ellipsis The grammatically allowed omission of one or more words from a sentence, where the words omitted can be precisely reconstructed. For example:

(a) *That car is older than this* ˆ.

(b) *Have you seen Samantha? No, I haven't* ˆ.

(c) *The children have travelled more widely than their parents* ˆ.

(d) *Boys will be boys,* and *girls* ˆ *girls.*

(Note that ˆ shows the point at which ellipsis occurs.) These examples show (a) ellipsis of a noun, (b) ellipsis of a **predication**, (c) ellipsis of a **predicate**, and (d) ellipsis of a **verb phrase**. Usually, as in these examples, the words omitted can be reconstructed because the same words occur in the context. For example, in (a) the ellipsis avoids the repetition of the word *car*. In avoiding repetition, ellipsis is similar in its function to **substitution** (e.g., the use of **pro-forms** such as *one* and *do so*), and is sometimes referred to as 'substitution by **zero**'.

embedding (or nesting) The inclusion of one unit as part of another unit of the same general type. For example, embedding of one **phrase** inside another is very common. In [*at* [*the other end* [*of* [*the road*]]]], one **prepositional phrase** [*of the road*] is embedded in another [*at the other end of the road*]; also, one **noun**

phrase [*the road*] is embedded in another noun phrase [*the other end of the road*]. Another major type of embedding is that of subordination of clauses – the inclusion of one clause (a **subordinate clause**) inside another one (the **main clause**). Embedding is one of the two devices of grammar which enable us to construct sentences which are as complex as we want – the other device being **coordination**.

emphasis A word referring generally to prominence given to one part of an utterance rather than another, e.g., by the use of stress, intonation, or particular words. In grammar, the term 'emphasis' has no precise meaning. However, we can note a number of emphatic grammatical devices, such as word order (see **end-focus**), the emphatic use of *do* (see **operator**), the emphatic use of reflexive pronouns (e.g., *the President himself*) (see **reflexive pronoun**), and the use of **degree adverbs** such as *so* and *absolutely* (e.g., *it's so/absolutely unfair!*) (see **intensification**). Emotive emphasis can be conveyed also by **interjections** and **exclamations**.

end-focus The principle by which elements placed towards the end of a phrase, clause or sentence tend to receive the focus or prominence associated with new information (see **given and new information**). Compare:

    (a) *I'm giving Mildred this dress.*
    (b) *I'm giving this dress to Mildred.*

Sentences (a) and (b) suggest different situations: in (a) 'this dress' is new information – the speaker may be showing the dress to a friend for the first time; in (b) 'to Mildred' is new information – the hearer may be looking at the dress already, but Mildred is now being mentioned, for the first time, as its recipient. Thus, in both cases, there is a tendency to put new information in a position of prominence at the end.

End-focus is important to grammar, because it helps to explain why, where grammar offers a choice of different **word-orders**, we choose one order rather than another. An example is the choice between active and **passive**. In spoken language, end-focus tends to coincide with intonational emphasis. Compare **end-weight**.

end-weight In grammar, the principle by which longer and more complex units tend to occur later in the sentence than shorter and less complex units. For example, in sentences consisting of **subject**, **verb phrase** and **object**, the subject is likely to be short and simple in comparison with the object. Where English grammar allows a choice of different word orders, end-weight helps to explain the choice of one order rather than another. For example, we can vary the order of the particle and object in a **phrasal verb** construction such as *put* (something) *off*. When the object is a **personal pronoun**, the order **object + particle** is always preferred, as in *They put it off*. If the object is a longer noun phrase, e.g., *the meeting*, then both orders can be used:

They put the meeting off ~ They put off the meeting.

When the object is even longer and more complex, the position object + particle becomes increasingly unacceptable, because of an increasing violation of the end-weight principle:

(a) *They put the next meeting of the General Assembly off.*

(b) *They put off the next meeting of the General Assembly.*

The order of (b) is clearly much more acceptable than that of (a). End-weight is closely related to **end-focus**.

exclamation   A kind of utterance which has as its major function the expression of strong feeling. Exclamations can vary from single exclamatory words such as *Oh!* (see **interjection**) to sentences with a full clause structure, including a verb phrase, as in *It's so absurd!* English has a special exclamatory sentence structure, beginning with *what* or *how*:

> (a) *What a strange sight they saw!*
> (b) *How lovely she looks!*

The element containing *what* or *how* may, for example, be an object, as in (a), or a complement, as in (b). The rest of the main clause follows, usually in its normal statement order: e.g., in (a) the order is object + subject + verb phrase; in (b) the order is complement + subject + verb phrase. The rest of the clause, after the **wh-element**, is often omitted, so that a verbless sentence results: *What a strange sight! How lovely!* A final exclamation mark (*!*) is the typical signal of an exclamation in writing. (See **sentence types**.) Compare **statement**; **question**.

exclamatory clause   see **clause**

exclamatory question   A kind of *yes–no* **question** having the force of an **exclamation**. Exclamatory questions are often negative in form, and are spoken with falling intonation, rather than with the rising intonation associated with ordinary *yes–no* questions: *Isn't this fun!* or (of someone else's children) *Haven't they grown!*

exclusive *we*   see **inclusive *we***

existential clause or **sentence** A **clause** or **simple sentence** with existential *there* as **subject**.

existential *there* The word *there* used as a dummy subject at the beginning of a clause or sentence, as in:

(a) *There will be trouble.*
(b) *There's nothing happening tonight.*
(c) *There were too many people in the room.*
(d) *There has been a lot of money wasted.*

Existential *there* is so called because it introduces sentences which postulate the existence of some state of affairs. Normally the sentence has *be* as its **main verb**. Existential *there*, unlike *there* as an adverb of place, is unstressed. The noun phrase following *be* can be seen as a delayed **subject**, and *there* as a dummy subject, inserted to fill the vacant initial subject position. Compare (d), for example, with the more standard word order of: *A lot of money has been wasted.* The delayed subject is usually indefinite in meaning, and sometimes shows its subject status by determining whether the verb phrase is singular or plural (see **concord**): compare (c) above with *There was too much noise in the room.* Nevertheless, in other ways, the status of subject belongs to *there*. For example, *there* comes after the **operator** in questions (*Is there anything happening?*) and occurs as matching subject in tag questions (*There's plenty of food left, isn't there?*) Hence the question of what is the subject of an existential sentence is problematic.

extraposition A special construction in which a **subordinate clause**, acting as **subject** of a **main clause**, is 'extraposed' – i.e.

placed at the end of the clause – and replaced by *it* as an initial subject:

> (a) [*That the expedition failed*] *was a pity.* ~
> (b) *It was a pity* [*that the expedition failed*].

Sentence (a) illustrates the normal subject–verb order, and (b) illustrates extraposition.

Not only a ***that*-clause**, but any kind of **nominal clause** can be 'extraposed' in this way. For example, an infinitive clause is extraposed in:

> (c) *It pays **to send your kids to a good school**.*

It is obvious that extraposition serves the purposes of **end-weight** and **end-focus**. Thus (c) would be an extremely awkward violation of end-weight if the normal subject–predicate order were used: *To send your kids to a good school pays.*

feminine   Having female, rather than male, reference (contrast **masculine**). Feminine and masculine forms traditionally make up the grammatical category of **gender**. In English grammar, the feminine gender is marked only in third-person singular **pronouns**: *she*, *her*, *hers* and *herself* are feminine pronouns. (Some nouns are also marked as having female reference by the ending *-ess*, e.g., *princess, goddess, lioness*.) (See **masculine; personal pronoun**.)

finite   see **finite verb**

finite auxiliary   see **operator**

finite clause   A **clause** which has a **finite verb**. For example, in

*When he's working, he **likes** us to be left alone*, the subordinate clause *when he's working* is a finite clause, likewise the main clause, which has *likes* as its verb phrase. But the infinitive clause *to be left alone* is non-finite. (See **finite verb; non-finite clause; verb phrase**.)

finite nominal clauses   see **nominal clause; reported speech**

finite verb   The form of a **verb** which varies for **present** and **past tense**. Hence finite verbs are sometimes called 'tensed' verbs. Both **auxiliaries** and **main verbs** have finite forms: e.g., *is ~ was ~ are ~ were, has ~ have ~ had, does ~ do ~ did, sees ~ see ~ saw, makes ~ make ~ made, listens ~ listen ~ listened*. Note that the **base form** of a verb is finite when it is used as a present tense form, but non-finite when it is used as an infinitive. Similarly, the *-ed* form of regular verbs is finite when it is used as a past tense form and non-finite when it is used as an *-ed* participle (past participle). **Modal auxiliaries** (e.g., *can, could, may, might, must*) are considered to be finite verbs, even though some of them lack a past tense form.

   Verb phrases are called finite when they begin with (or consist of) a finite verb: e.g., *works, is working, has worked; has been taking, was taken, was being taken* are all finite verb phrases. (See **finite clause; non-finite verb; past tense; present tense; verb phrase**.)

first person   see **imperative; person**

first person pronoun   A **pronoun** referring to the speaker or writer (with or without other people). The first person singular pronouns are *I*, *me*, *my*, *mine*, and *myself*. The first person plural pronouns are *we*, *us*, *our*, *ours*, *ourselves*. (See **person**; **personal pronoun**; **reflexive pronoun**.)

foreign plural nouns Nouns which have been borrowed into English from other languages and which form their **plural** on the pattern of the foreign (or classical) language from which they come. For example:

> *stimulus ~ stimuli stratum ~ strata* (Latin)
>
> *axis ~ axes criterion ~ criteria* (Greek)
>
> *corps ~ corps rendezvous ~ rendezvous* (French)
>
> *virtuoso ~ virtuosi tempo ~ tempi* (Italian)
>
> *seraph ~ seraphim cherub ~ cherubim* (Hebrew)

Often a foreign noun can be used with a regular plural, as well as with its foreign plural. For instance, as the Latin plural of *index*, *indices* is used in technical contexts; but the regular plural *indexes* is preferred in everyday use, e.g., in referring to the indexes at the back of a book. (See **irregular plurals**; **plural**.)

formal and informal Terms used of 'higher' and 'lower' levels of style or usage in English. Formal style is associated with careful usage, especially written language, whereas informal style is associated with colloquial usage, especially spoken, conversational language in relaxed or private settings. Formal features of English grammar include the placing of **prepositions** before a **wh-word**, e.g., *To whom does the house belong?*, as contrasted with the more informal (and usual) *Who does the house belong to?* One feature of informal English grammar is the use of verb and negative **contractions**, e.g., *She's ill* (more formal: *She is ill*) and *couldn't* (more formal: *could not*). Formal grammar is more influenced by the tradition of Latin-based grammar: e.g., the pronoun *I* is formal in **comparative** constructions such as *My brother was taller than I*, as contrasted with *My brother was taller than me*.

formulaic subjunctive see **subjunctive**

frequency adverb/adverbial An **adverb, adverbial** phrase, or **adverbial clause** which indicates how often an event takes place. For example: *rarely* in *We **rarely** meet nowadays* is a frequency adverb. Other examples are *always, usually, frequently, often, sometimes, occasionally, never, hardly ever, every year, twice a week, whenever I write to her*. Frequency adverbials answer the question 'How often?' or 'How many times?'

front-position The position of an **adverbial** when it occurs at the beginning of a **clause**, before the **subject**. For example, *Normally* in (a) and *On Sunday* in (b) are in front-position:

    (a) ***Normally**, the train arrives on time.*
    (b) ***On Sunday**, we said goodbye to all our neighbours.*

function words (or **grammatical words**) Words whose role is chiefly to be explained in terms of the grammar of the language, rather than in terms of dictionary definition. Function words contrast with **lexical** or 'content words', such as **nouns** and **adjectives**. The main classes of function words are **determiners, prepositions, conjunctions, auxiliary verbs**, and **pronouns**. (See **open and closed word classes**.)

future constructions Grammatical word-combinations used in referring to future time. In English, the **modal** *will* is the most common way of referring to things happening in the future, e.g., *The Women's Final **will take** place next Saturday.* The *will* + infinitive construction is sometimes called the 'future tense', but it is not comparable to the **past tense** and **present tense**, which are indicated by morphological forms of the verb word itself (e.g., *work*[*s*] and *worked*, in contrast to the future construction *will work*). *Will* has its own past tense form *would*, which can indicate 'future-in-the-past', as in *Susan was glad that her journey **would** soon be over.* Also, combined with the **perfect** *have* + *ed*-form, *will* can indicate 'past-in-the-future', e.g., *This time next week we **will have finished** our exams.* Apart from *will*, there are a number of other ways of indicating the future in English. The most common are:

> *be going to* – *I'm **going to** buy you a present.*
> **Present progressive** – *She's **meeting** me tomorrow.*
> **Present simple** (especially in **subordinate clauses**) – *Phone us when you **arrive** this evening.*
> *will* + **progressive** – *Next week's programme **will be starting** half an hour earlier.*
> *shall* + **infinitive** (in **formal** style, with **first person** subjects) – *We **shall look** forward to receiving your order.*

(See **modal auxiliary; past tense; present tense.**)

future perfect The **verb** construction consisting of *will* + perfect infinitive (e.g., *will have eaten*), referring to something which, from a future standpoint, is seen to have happened in the past. (See **future constructions; perfect.**)

gender The grammatical category which distinguishes **masculine,**

feminine, and **neuter** (or non-personal) pronouns. In English grammar, gender is limited to third-person singular **personal** and **reflexive pronouns**: *he*, *him*, *his*, and *himself* are masculine; *she*, *her*, *hers*, and *herself* are feminine; and *it*, *its*, *itself* are neuter. Gender has been a prominent issue in discussions of grammar in recent years: since English lacks a singular personal pronoun which is neutral between male and female reference, it has been felt desirable to avoid the traditional masculine bias of generic *he*, for example, by using *he or she*, or *they*. Compare:

(a) *Everyone thinks **he** has the answer.*
(b) *Everyone thinks **he or she** has the answer.*
(c) *Everyone thinks **they** have the answer.*

In recent years, for sex-neutral reference, the use of (a) *he* has declined, whereas the use of (b) *he or she*, and (c) *they* has increased. However, the use of *they* in examples like (c) causes controversy, because it is felt to be a breach of **concord**. (See **feminine**; **masculine**; **personal pronoun**.)

generic Referring to a whole class, rather than to individual members of a class. For example, the subjects of (a), (b), and (c) are generic (referring to computers in general):

(a) ***The computer** is a remarkable machine.*
(b) ***A computer** is a remarkable machine.*
(c) ***Computers** are remarkable machines.*

In contrast, the subjects of (d) and (e) are not generic, since they refer to an individual computer:

(d) ***The computer** isn't working: it needs repair.*

(e) *A computer has been stolen from the laboratory.*

Note that the **definite** and **indefinite articles** (*the* and *a*) are generic in some contexts and specific in others. The articles are usually specific in meaning, but when *the* comes before an **adjective** as **head** of the noun phrase, it is normally generic: *the rich*, *the unemployed*, *the absurd*.

genitive   The form of a **noun** or **noun phrase** ending in *'s* (apostrophe *s*) or *s'* (*s* apostrophe), and indicating possession or some such meaning. (Apart from a few special cases, the *s'* spelling is restricted to the genitive ending of regular plural nouns, such as *boys* ~ *boys'*.) The genitive form of a noun typically comes before another noun, the head of the noun phrase of which the genitive is part, e.g., *Robert's desk*. Historically, the genitive is the only remnant in modern English of the **case** system of nouns, prevalent in Old English, and also in classical Greek, Latin and many modern European languages. The *of*-phrase (sometimes called the '*of*-genitive') has replaced the genitive in many usages; in others, both constructions can be used, e.g., *the arrival of the bride = the bride's arrival*. In modern English, the genitive is strictly speaking no longer a case-ending at all: rather, it is an ending added to noun phrases, such as [*the bride's*] in [*the bride's*] *arrival* above, or [*my father's*] in [*my father's*] *favourite breakfast*. Note that *my* belongs with *father's* in this example, rather than with *breakfast*.

The genitive fills a **determiner** slot in the larger noun phrase of which it is part: hence the function of *the bride's* above is similar to that of *her* in *her arrival*, or *the* in *the arrival*. Potentially, the genitive may be quite a complicated **phrase**. But there is a tendency to prefer the *of*-construction where the genitive would cause too much complexity in front of the noun. Hence *the night train to Edinburgh's departure* is less likely to occur than *the departure of the night train to Edinburgh*. Notice, in this example, however, that the placing of the *'s* at the end of *Edinburgh* is perfectly acceptable, even though the genitive indicates the train's departure, rather than the departure of Edinburgh! This is an example of the so-called group genitive, where the genitive phrase contains postmodification. Other examples are: [*the mayor of Chicago's*] *re-election campaign*, [*someone else's*] *fault*. Although such examples are possible, however, the most common type of genitive consists of just one noun: a proper noun, and particularly the name of a person: [*Napoleon's*] *horse*, [*Marion's*] *husband*, etc. Sometimes the noun following the genitive is omitted: *This scarf must be your sister's*. The genitive forms of personal pronouns (e.g., *my*, *your*, *his*) are known as possessive pronouns. (See case; possessive pronoun.)

genitive nouns   see possessive pronouns

gerund   A traditional term used in reference to the *-ing* form of a verb when it has a noun-like function. In this book, *-ing* form is a general term for words called either 'gerund' or 'present participle' in traditional approaches to grammar.

get-passive   see passive

given and new information   A classification of the information conveyed by a sentence, clause, or other grammatical unit. Given information is information already assumed to be known by the audience or reader; and new information is information not previously known, and therefore to be particularly brought to the hearer's or reader's attention. In speech, new information is signalled by intonation and stress. For example, in the following exchange, the words in capitals represent important new information, and are also the words which are likely to be strongly stressed:

(a) *Will the match take place* TOMORROW?

(b) *Well, it* MAY *do, but I hope it will be* POSTPONED.

There is a tendency to place new information after given information, i.e. to save up the important new information to the end of a sentence or clause. However, a speaker can vary the position of old and new information, by varying the position of stress. Notice, for example, the difference of effect between (a) above, and the same sentence (c) with a different major stress:

(c) *Will the match take* PLACE *tomorrow?*

(See **end-focus**.)

gradable adjectives see **adjective**; **gradable word**

gradable word   A word which can easily be used in the **comparative** or **superlative**, or is capable of being modified by an adverb of **degree** such as *very, much, greatly, considerably, rather* and *little*. For example, the adjectives *tall* and *beautiful* are gradable, because they have comparative and superlative forms (*taller* ~ *tallest, more beautiful* ~ *most beautiful*), also because they can be modified by *very*, etc.: *very tall, very beautiful*. In contrast, the adjectives *double* and *female* are non-gradable, since we cannot normally say *doubler, *more female, *very double, *rather female, etc. Many **adjectives** are gradable, and so are some **adverbs** and **determiners** (e.g., *often, easily, many, much*). Sometimes the same word may be gradable in one context but not in another. For example, *human* in *a human being* or *human history* is non-gradable. But we can say of a dog that its behaviour is *very human*, meaning that it behaves very much like a human being.

grammatical form   see **notional concord**

grammatical words   see **function words**; compare **lexical** words.

group genitive   see **genitive**

group noun   An alternative name for **collective noun.**

head   The main word in a **phrase**. The head of a **noun phrase** is (normally) a **noun** or a **pronoun**. The head of an **adjective phrase** is an **adjective**. The head of an **adverb phrase** is an **adverb**. The head of a phrase is an obligatory element, and other words, phrases, or clauses are optionally added to it to qualify its meaning. These optional elements are called **modifiers**. For example, in (*friendly*) *places* (*to stay*), (*extremely*) *tall*, and (*more*) *often* (*than I expected*), the parts in parentheses are modifiers, and those not in parentheses are the heads of their phrases. (In this book we do not talk of heads and modifiers in verb phrases and prepositional phrases, but in some versions of grammar these phrases are also analysed in terms of heads and modifiers.) (See **modifier; phrase.**)

historic present   The use of the **present tense** in referring to past time, e.g., *A few weeks ago, I'm looking out of the window and suddenly a strange object comes into view*. The historic present is sometimes used to create a vivid impression in popular oral narrative, and also occasionally in novels and short stories.

hypothetical   see **past tense; subjunctive**

hypothetical past   The use of the **past tense** to refer to an event or state of affairs which is not real. The event or state is seen as happening in some imaginary circumstance (past, present or future), rather than in the world of fact, for example, in unreal **conditional clauses**: *If the principal knew about it, she would be furious*. The implication of this sentence is that the principal does *not* know about it. The past **modal auxiliaries** are often hypothetical, e.g., *I couldn't live with a man like that: it would be a nightmare*. To combine hypothetical meaning with past time, we use the **past perfect**: *I would have helped you last week if you had asked me*. This implies that 'you did *not* ask me'. (See **past tense**.)

if-clause   see **conditional clause**

imperative   A form of the verb used to express a command or directive, i.e. something which the speaker requires the hearer to do. For this purpose, English always uses the **base form** of the **verb** (the form without any ending or inflection), e.g., *take*, *look*, *send*, *let*, *prepare*. The imperatives of the **primary verbs** are *be*, *have*, and *do*. When used for commands, the imperative can be impolite: *Sit down*; *Come here*. This can be made slightly more polite by adding *please*: *Please sit down*; *Come here, please*.

However, the imperative can also be used politely for invitations, good wishes, etc.: *Take a look at this!*; *Have a good time!*; *Enjoy yourselves*. To make a negative imperative, we add *Don't* at the beginning: *Don't be silly*; *Don't make a mess*. In addition, we can add the emphatic auxiliary *Do* at the beginning, to make the imperative more insistent or persuasive in tone: *Do make yourself comfortable* is an insistent invitation.

The term imperative is used not only for the imperative verb itself but for a sentence having such a verb. Imperative sentences normally have no **subject**, but the implied subject is *you*, as we see when the reflexive pronoun *yourself* or *yourselves* is used as an object: *Behave yourself*; *Make yourselves at home*. In exceptional cases, we use *you* (stressed) as subject: *You be quiet*. Occasionally other subjects (such as names or indefinite pronouns) are also used: *Everyone sit down*; *Somebody make a cup of tea*. Another form of imperative has the initial word *Let's*: *Let's go for a swim*. This is a first-person imperative, including both the speaker and the hearer in the suggested action.

imperative clause   see **clause**

inclusive we   The use of *we* to include reference to the hearer(s), as well as the speaker. For example, *we* means 'you and I' in *You and I must have a talk. When shall we meet?* If *we* does not have this meaning, it is termed 'exclusive' (exclusive **we**), as in: *We look forward to seeing you* (where *we* = 'the speaker and others'). (See **first person pronouns**.)

indefinite article   The word *a* (before consonants) or *an* (before vowels). *A/an* is only used with singular **count nouns** (compare **zero**

article). It is a **determiner**, and normally occurs at the beginning of a **noun phrase**. As indefinite article, *a/an* contrasts with the **definite article** *the*: it is used to introduce a noun phrase referring to something or somebody who has not been mentioned or whose identity is not yet known to one's hearer or reader. For instance: *I've just bought a car*; *Do you have a box of matches?*; *An old friend of mine lives here. A/an* is also used (e.g., after *be*) to describe or classify people or objects: *My mother's a teacher*; *An arquebus is an old-fashioned gun.* Historically, *a/an* is a reduced form of the word *one*, and it is often used instead of *one* in expressions like *a hundred, an hour and a half*, etc. (See **articles**; **generic**.)

indefinite pronoun, indefinite determiner A **pronoun** or **determiner** with indefinite meaning; a quantifier. The indefinite pronouns and determiners in English are:

PRONOUNS

anybody	*everybody*	*nobody*	*somebody*
anyone	*everyone*	*no one*	*someone*
anything	*everything*	*nothing*	*something*
none			

DETERMINERS

a/an every no

BOTH PRONOUNS AND DETERMINERS
*any all both each either enough (a) few fewer fewest half
(a) little less least many more most much neither one
several some*

independent and dependent clauses An independent clause is one which is not part of (i.e. is not subordinate to) another clause. For example, in the coordinate sentence:

(a) [*He scored a goal*], *and* [*everybody cheered*].

both the clauses linked by *and* are independent. But in the sentence:

(b) [[*When he scored the goal*], *everybody cheered*].

the clause beginning with *when* is dependent, being an **adverbial** part of the main (independent) clause. In the sentence:

(c) [$_1$ *I thought* [$_2$ *that he was joking* [$_3$ *when he said that* $_3$]$_2$]$_1$], *but* [$_4$ *I was wrong* $_4$].

clauses 2 and 3 are dependent clauses, but clauses 1 and 4 are independent. Compare **main clause; subordinate clause.**

indicative mood   see **mood**

indirect object   An **object** noun phrase which normally follows the **main verb**, and precedes the **direct object**. For example:

*They gave **the children** a beautiful present.*
*I'm going to cook **you all** a light lunch.*

The indirect object usually refers to someone indirectly affected by the action of the verb, e.g., a recipient or beneficiary. The same idea can often be expressed by a phrase beginning with *to* or *for*: *They gave a present **to the children**; I'm going to cook lunch **for you all***. The indirect object can become the subject of a **passive**: *The children were given a beautiful present.* (See **direct object; object.**)

indirect speech   see **reported speech**

infinitive   The **base form** of the **verb** (i.e. the form without any suffix or inflection) used as a **non-finite verb**. For example *be, have, do, see, regret* are infinitives when they follow a **modal auxiliary** or *do*: *may **be**, could **have**, can't **do**, might **see**, don't regret*. Also, the infinitive is used as the verb (or first verb) of a **non-finite clause**, where it is often preceded by *to*:

> *They want **to** be met at the station.*
> ***To** have escaped alive was an amazing achievement.*

The term infinitive is used (a) for the verb form itself (e.g., *be, have*), (b) for the **verb phrase** (e.g., *to be met, to have escaped*), and (c) for the **clause** (e.g., *to be met at the station, to have escaped alive*) which has the infinitive verb phrase. (See **bare infinitive; non-finite verb**; *to*-**infinitive**.)

infinitive clauses   see **infinitive; non-finite clause**; *to*-**infinitive**

inflection (or **inflexion**)   A change in the form of a word, which signals a different grammatical function of the same word. The regular inflections in English are endings (suffixes) such as *-ed, -(e)s*, or *-ing* added to the **base form** of a regular verb: *want, wanted, wants, wanting*. Other inflections take the form of a change of vowel, with or without the addition of a suffix: e.g., in the irregular verb *take, took* and *taken* are the **past tense** and **-ed participle** forms. We distinguish inflectional suffixes from derivational suffixes, which derive one word from another. For example, the *-s* of *boys* is inflectional, forming the **plural** of the same noun. But the *-ish* of *boyish* is derivational, forming another word (an **adjective**) from the noun *boy*. (See **irregular plurals; irregular verbs.**)

inflectional morphology   see **morphology**

inflexion   see **inflection**

informal   see **formal and informal**

information (packaging)   see **given and new information**

***-ing* clause**   A type of **clause** in which the first (or only) **verb** word is an ***-ing* form**: *coming home*; *not doing the job properly*; *having been a teacher*; *visiting the park*. All *-ing* clauses are **non-finite clauses**, normally **subordinate** to other clauses. They have varied functions:

(a) *We met a lot of traffic [**coming home**].*
(b) *He was accused of [**not doing the job properly**].*
(c) *[**Having been a teacher**], you will know what kids are like.*
(d) *The people [**visiting the park**] enjoy [**walking among the flower beds**].*

In (a), *coming home* is an **adverbial clause** (of time). In (b), the *-ing* clause is a **nominal clause**. In (c) *Having been a teacher* is again an adverbial clause (of **cause or reason**). In (d), the first *-ing* clause is an **adjectival clause**, similar to the **relative clause** *who visit the park*, and the second is a nominal clause, acting as **object** of *enjoy*. Although a typical *-ing* clause usually has no **subject**, its implied subject is usually clear from the context. Sometimes, however, we place an overt subject in front of the *-ing* form:

57

(e) *I'm fed up with* [*these trains being late*].

(f) [*Weather permitting*], *the competition will be held in the open.*

In more **formal** English, the subject of a nominal *-ing* clause is sometimes a genitive or a possessive pronoun: *The flight delay was due to* [*its being the peak holiday season*]. An *-ing* clause is sometimes called a 'present participle construction' (especially when it is adjectival, as in (d)), or a 'gerund(ival) construction' (when it is nominal). (See **-ing form; non-finite clause.**)

-ing form   The form of the **verb** ending in *-ing*, e.g., *being, doing, sending, increasing*. It is a non-finite form of the verb, and is added to *be* to make the **progressive** construction: *is eating, were making, has been increasing*, etc. It can also be used as the only (or first) word of a **verb phrase**, and as the first word of an **-ing clause**: [*Buying clothes*] *is what I hate most*; *She loves* [*being taken to the races*]. The *-ing* form is sometimes called a 'present participle' or (when it is in a **nominal clause**) a 'gerund'. The *-ing* form, as a form of a verb, should be distinguished from nouns and adjectives ending in *-ing* (e.g., a new *building*, an *interesting* book).

instrument adverb/adverbial   see **adjunct; adverbial**

intensification   A general term for the use of **degree adverbs** or **adverbials** to intensify the meaning of some part of a sentence. This can apply to the intensification of **adjectives** and **adverbs** (*immensely hot, very occasionally*), and also, for example, to the intensification of **negative words** and **question words**: *I'm not in the least hungry; What on earth were you thinking about?* Compare **emphasis.**

intensifier   An alternative term for an **adverb** of **degree**, especially one which intensifies or strengthens the meaning of the word it modifies (e.g., *very*, *extremely*, *really*).

interjection   A word which has a purely exclamatory function, such as *oh*, *ah*, *aha*, *ugh*, *ooh*, *alas*, *hey*. Interjections do not refer to anything, but simply express the speaker's emotion or wish. In grammatical terms, they occur in isolation, as an **exclamation**, or are loosely added on to a sentence, as in *Oh, it was wonderful!*

interrogative   Having a **question** function. The main types of interrogative sentences are **yes–no questions**, **wh-questions**, and **alternative questions**. (Subordinate interrogative clauses are discussed under **wh-clause** and **reported speech**. Interrogative words are discussed under **wh-word**.) (See **question**.)

interrogative clause   see **clause**

intransitive   see **transitive verb**

intransitive verb   A **verb** which does not require any **object, complement**, or other element to complete its meaning. Thus, to complete a sentence, an intransitive verb can be added to the **subject**, without any further addition: *Everyone laughed*; *The snow is falling*. But **adverbial** elements can be freely added after the intransitive verb: *Everyone laughed at the joke*; *The snow is falling heavily in the north*. (See **transitive verb**; **verb pattern**.)

introductory *it*, introductory *there*   *It* and *there* used as introductory

subjects in certain special kinds of sentence pattern. (See **cleft sentence; existential** *there*; **extraposition**.)

inversion   The reversal of the normal order of **subject** and **verb** word, so that the verb word precedes the subject. In English, we distinguish two kinds of inversion. Subject–operator inversion occurs where the **operator** (an **auxiliary verb** or the main verb *be*) is placed before the subject, e.g., in **questions**, or in **statements** introduced by a **negative word**:

> *The weather is improving* ∼ *Is the weather improving?*
> *He did not say a word* ∼ *Not a word did he say.*

Subject–verb inversion occurs when the **main verb** (often the verb *be* or a simple verb of position or motion) is placed before the subject, in limited circumstances, especially when an adverbial of place introduces the sentence:

> *Your sister is there* ∼ *There's your sister.*
> *The rain came down* ∼ *Down came the rain.*
> *The old city lies beneath the castle ramparts* ∼ *Beneath the castle ramparts lies the old city.*

(See *wh*-**question**; *yes–no* **question**.)

irregular plurals   Noun **plurals** which do not follow the regular pattern of adding -(*e*)*s* to the singular. Common examples are:

man ∼ men	*foot ∼ feet*	*sheep ∼ sheep*	*wife ∼ wives*
woman ∼ women	*tooth ∼ teeth*	*deer ∼ deer*	*life ∼ lives*
child ∼ children	*goose ∼ geese*	*mouse ∼ mice*	*leaf ∼ leaves*
ox ∼ oxen			

These are 'native' plurals, relics of an earlier stage of the English language. In addition, there are 'foreign' irregular plurals, such as those borrowed from Latin and Greek, e.g., *stratum ~ strata*. (See **foreign plurals**; **plural**.)

irregular verbs Verb words which do not form their **past tense** and **-ed participle** form in the regular way (see **verb**). There are over 200 irregular verbs in English, including many of the most common and important verbs in the language. In the following examples, (1) is the **base form**, (2) is the past tense form, and (3) is the -ed participle form:

(1)	(2)	(3)	(1)	(2)	(3)
be	~ was/were	~ been	bring	~ brought	~ brought
come	~ came	~ come	do	~ did	~ done
eat	~ ate	~ eaten	feel	~ felt	~ felt
give	~ gave	~ given	go	~ went	~ gone
have	~ had	~ had	know	~ knew	~ known
let	~ let	~ let	make	~ made	~ made
put	~ put	~ put	run	~ ran	~ run
say	~ said	~ said	see	~ saw	~ seen
sit	~ sat	~ sat	stand	~ stood	~ stood
tell	~ told	~ told	think	~ thought	~ thought

All English **auxiliary verbs** are irregular, and the verb *be*, the most common verb of English, is the most irregular of all. It has eight forms: *am*, *is*, *are*, *was*, *were*, *be*, *being*, *been*.

levels of style or usage   see **formal and informal**

lexical Relating to the lexicon (i.e. the dictionary, or the vocabulary) of a language. A rough distinction is sometimes made between lexical words (or content words), whose meaning is explained in terms of their lexical content, and grammatical words (or **function words**), whose role is chiefly to be explained in terms of the grammar of a language. For example, **nouns** are lexical words, and **articles** are grammatical words. The term lexical verb is sometimes used for **main verbs**, as contrasted with **auxiliary verbs**.

linking adverbial (also called **conjunct**) An **adverbial** element whose main function is to link two sentences, clauses, etc. together. Examples are: *however, nevertheless* (both expressing contrast), *moreover* (expressing addition), *otherwise* (expressing an alternative), *meanwhile* (expressing a link of time). These are all single-word adverbials, i.e. **adverbs**, but in other cases a linking adverbial may be a phrase or even a clause. For example, instead of *nevertheless*, we can use *all the same* or *in spite of that*, or instead of *moreover*, we can use *what is more*. Linking adverbials usually occur at the beginning of the sentence etc., that they link, but unlike coordinating **conjunctions** (such as *and, or,* and *but*) they may occur also in the middle or at the end. All three of the following (a)–(c) might come after the sentence *Jason supports the animal rights campaign*:

(a) *However, his father disagrees with him.*
(b) *His father, however, disagrees with him.*
(c) *His father disagrees with him, however.*

linking verb (also called **copulative** or **copular verb**) A **main verb**

which, like the verb *be*, links a subject to a subject complement. *Be* is by far the most common linking verb, and is called the **copula**:

> *Those cakes **are** delicious.*
> *The meeting **was** a great success.*

Other linking verbs add an extra meaning to the neutral meaning of *be*:

> *Those cakes **look** delicious.*
> *The meeting **proved** a great success.*

Some other linking verbs are: ***sound**, **feel**, **smell**, **taste**, **appear**, **seem**, **become**, **get**, **go**, **grow**, **turn***. Note that *be*, and some other linking verbs, can also be followed by an **adverbial**:

> *The meeting **will be** at five o'clock.*
> *Everyone **will be** there.*

linking words A general term for words which have a linking role in grammar, such as **conjunctions**, **linking adverbials** and **linking verbs**.

main clause A clause which has another **clause** (known as a **subordinate clause**) as part of it. For example, in

> [*The whole world hopes* [*that peace will prevail*]*.*]

the outer parentheses enclose the main clause, and the inner brackets enclose another clause, a subordinate clause. The subordinate clause is part of the main clause. The following is a slightly more complex sentence, in which there are three clauses, one inside the other:

[₁ *I wonder* [₂ *if you could tell me* [₃ *how she is* ₃]₂].₁]

The clause marked 1 is definitely a main clause, and the clause marked 3 is definitely a subordinate clause. But clause 2 is both a main clause and a subordinate clause: it is a main clause when we look at it in relation to clause 3, and a subordinate clause when we look at it in relation to clause 1. In other words, we interpret main clause and subordinate clause as relative terms. Contrast **independent and dependent clauses**. (See **subordinate clause**.)

main verb A verb word which is not an **auxiliary verb**, and which must occur in any normal clause or sentence (but see **verbless clause; ellipsis**). In the following examples, the word in *italics* is the main verb:

came	*takes*	*is*
has *come*	are *taking*	*being*
has been *coming*	having been *taken*	may have *been*

Note that the auxiliary verbs – those not in italics – always come before the main verb. Note also that the primary verbs *be*, *have*, and *do* can be either an auxiliary or a main verb. When they are main verbs, they are the last (or only) verb in the **verb phrase**. Hence, in *Jack is asleep* or *Jack may have been asleep*, *be* is the main verb; but in *Jack is lying* or *Jack may have been lying*, *lie* is the main verb and *be* an auxiliary. The main verb is a pivotal word, to a great extent determining the structural and meaning relations within the clause. The term '**lexical** verb' is sometimes used instead of main verb, but strictly speaking, 'lexical verb' excludes the primary verbs *be*, **have** and **do** even when they act as main verbs. (See **auxiliary verb**.)

mandative subjunctive   see **subjunctive**

manner adverb/adverbial   An **adverb(ial)** whose meaning is 'in such-and-such a manner'. The most common manner adverbials are adverbs derived from **adjectives**, typically ending in *-ly*, e.g., *badly, slowly, hungrily, unconsciously*, etc. Manner adverbs which are irregular in this respect are *well* (= 'good + ly'), *better, best, worse* (= 'more badly'), and *worst*, as in *Paula plays the guitar well. Of the three children, Paula plays the guitar best/worst.* Manner adverbials answer the question 'How?'

masculine   Having male, rather than female, reference (contrast **feminine**). Masculine, feminine and **neuter** forms traditionally make up the grammatical category of **gender**. However, gender has only a limited role in English grammar, being restricted to the third-person pronouns. The masculine pronouns in English are *he, him, his* and *himself.* (See **feminine; personal pronoun**.)

mass noun   A **noun** which refers to substances (solids, liquids, and gases) in the mass, c.g., *rice, milk, tar, smoke*. Mass nouns are **non-count nouns**. (See **count noun; non-count noun**.)

means adverb/adverbial   see **adverbial**

mid-position   The position in which an **adverbial** is placed when it occurs in the middle of a clause. For example, the adverbs are in mid-position in: *The game will **soon** begin*; *Our friends **often** send us presents*; *The children were **fortunately** in bed.* The most usual mid-position is (a) just after the **operator**, if any; (b) otherwise just after the **subject**.

modal (auxiliary) (verb) A member of a small class of **verbs** which have meanings relating to modality, i.e. to such concepts as possibility or permission (*can*, *may*), obligation, necessity, or likelihood (*must*, *should*), prediction, intention or hypothesis (*will*, *would*). The modal auxiliaries group in pairs, except for *must*:

> will   can   may   shall   must
> would could might should

The lower modals are historically the past tense forms of the upper modals, but nowadays they have developed independent uses (especially *would* and *should*). The modals always function as **operators**, and occur in first position in their **verb phrase**. They form a construction with the bare infinitive of another verb, e.g., *may be*, *may have*, *may find*. They have no other forms, such as *-s* forms, *-ing* forms, or *-ed* forms. They are placed before the subject to form **questions**, and before *not* in **negation**:

QUESTION	NEGATION

You can help me ~ *Can you help me?* ~ *You cannot help me.*
We will succeed ~ *Will we succeed?* ~ *We will not succeed.*

Except for *may*, modals can also express negation by negative **contractions**: *won't*, *can't*, *shan't*, *mustn't*, *wouldn't*, *couldn't*, *mightn't*, *shouldn't*: *You **can't** help me*; *We **won't** succeed.* Modals are very widely used in conversation, for expressing various kinds of speech acts, such as requests (*Could I use your phone?*; *Would you mind signing this form?*) or offers (*Can we offer you a lift?*; *Shall I open the door for you?*). Some less important verbs (*ought to, used to, need, dare* are sometimes included with the modals because of their similar meanings and/or grammatical behaviour. (See **auxiliary verb; operator.**)

modality   see **modal; verb**

modifier   A word, phrase, or clause which is added to another word to specify more precisely what it refers to. For example, in the following phrases, the expressions in **bold** are modifiers:

   (a) *a **new** house **in the country*** **(noun phrase)**
   (b) *something **which I bought recently*** **(noun phrase)**
   (c) ***amazingly** beautiful* **(adjective phrase)**
   (d) *often **enough*** **(adverb phrase)**

The words *house, something, beautiful,* and *often* in these examples are termed the **heads** of their respective phrases. Modifiers preceding the head are called **premodifiers** (e.g., *new* in (a)). Modifiers following the head are called **postmodifiers** (e.g., *in the country* in (a)). In noun phrases, adjective phrases and adverb phrases, modifiers are optional elements which add specification to the meaning of the head.

mood   A **verb** category which is not so useful in the grammar of English as it is for some other languages, and has to do with the degree of reality attributed to the happening described by the verb. The indicative mood (that of normal finite forms of the verb) contrasts with the 'unreality' of the **subjunctive** mood. The **imperative** and **infinitive** are also sometimes considered to be moods of the verb.

morphology The part of grammar (and lexicology) which analyses the structure of words. Morphology is a relatively unimportant part of English grammar, because English words have relatively few inflections (i.e. changes in the form of words determined by their grammatical role). The suffixes of **nouns** (*-s*), **verbs** (*-ed, -ing, -s*) and **adjectives** (*-er, -est*) comprise an important part of morphology. Inflectional morphology is distinguished from derivational morphology, which deals with the formation of words, and belongs to lexicology rather than grammar. However, derivational morphology is relevant to grammar because derivational suffixes such as *-ness* (for nouns), *-ful* (for adjectives) and *-ly* (for adverbs) help us to recognize the members of grammatical word classes. Contrast **syntax**.

naming expression A word or phrase which refers to an individual person, place, group, etc. The simplest naming expressions are **proper nouns** such as *Jane, Robinson, Moscow, Africa*. Other naming expressions may contain sequences of such names (*Abraham Lincoln*), names preceded by titles (*Mrs Indira Gandhi*), names followed by common nouns (*the Atlas Mountains*), etc. Naming expressions are spelt with initial capitals on important (especially **lexical**) words, and are often reduced to initials or acronyms, e.g., *the UN, OPEC, NATO*.

nationality word A **noun** or **adjective** identifying one particular country or its inhabitants. For example, *Spain* (**proper noun**),

Spanish (**adjective**), *Spaniard* (**common noun** referring to an [especially male] individual of Spanish nationality). Nationality words are spelt with an initial capital letter, even when they are adjectives or common nouns.

negation The operation of changing a sentence or other unit into its negative form, especially by using *not*. The normal form of negation in English is to add *not* (or its contracted form *-n't*) after the **operator** (i.e. after the first **auxiliary verb** or the **finite verb** *be*):

POSITIVE	NEGATIVE
I am feeling tired	~ I am **not** feeling tired.
You could help her	~ You **couldn't** help her.
The letter is here	~ The letter **isn't** here.

When the positive sentence has no operator, *do* is used as a dummy operator to form the negative:

> Sue likes jogging ~ Sue **doesn't** like jogging.

The contracted negative forms can be used in informal style. They are: *isn't, aren't, wasn't, weren't, hasn't, haven't, hadn't, doesn't, don't, didn't, won't, shan't, can't, mustn't, wouldn't, shouldn't, couldn't, mightn't*. For some operators there is no negative contraction (e.g., *may not, am not*), and so the full form has to be used. In making a sentence or clause negative, we sometimes have to make other changes. Thus, it is common to replace *some* by *any* when it follows *not*: *We saw **some** rare birds ~ We didn't see **any** rare birds.* (See **negative word**; **non-assertive**; **transferred negation**.)

negative   see **negation**; **positive**

negative word   A word which has the function of negating the meaning of a clause or sentence. Apart from the most important negative word *not*, other negative words include *no* (**determiner**, or **response form**); *none, nobody, no one, nothing* (**pronouns**); *never, nowhere* (**adverbs**). The functions of these are similar to that of *not*: to say ***Nobody*** *was asleep* is to say the same as *Everyone was* ***not*** *asleep*, i.e. *Everyone was awake.* When a negative word comes later than the **subject** of the sentence, it can usually be replaced by *not* with a **non-assertive** word such as *any, anyone, ever*: *I have* ***never*** *learned to ski* = *I haven't* ***ever*** *learned to ski.*

nesting   see **embedding**

neuter (or non-personal)   Having neither **masculine** nor **feminine** gender. *It*, in contrast to *he* and *she*, is a neuter pronoun.

new information   see **given and new information**

nominal   The adjective corresponding to **noun**.

nominal clause (also called noun clause)   A **subordinate clause** which has a function in the sentence similar to that of a **noun phrase**. Like noun phrases, nominal clauses can act as **subject**, **object**, or **complement** of the main clause:

> [*What you do*] *does not concern me.*   (subject)
> *I didn't ask* [*where they live*].   (object)
> *The hope is* [*that we will succeed*].   (complement)

Some nominal clauses can also occur after a **preposition**: *It all depends on [how you feel]*. Finite nominal clauses include *that*-clauses, *wh*-interrogative clauses, and **nominal relative clauses**. There are also non-finite nominal clauses, e.g., the *-ing* clauses in *[Sending him money now] would be like [putting the cart before the horse]*.

nominal relative clause   A **relative clause** which has no **antecedent**, and which is therefore equivalent, in its function in the sentence, to a whole **noun phrase**, for example, *[What you need most] is a good stiff drink*. Here *What you need most* means the same as 'The thing which you need most'. Nominal relative clauses begin with a *wh*-word, often a *wh*-ever word like *whoever*: *I want to speak to [whoever answered the phone just now]* (i.e. 'the person who answered the phone just now').

nominalization   A **noun phrase** which has the underlying semantic structure of a **clause**. An example of nominalization is *the destruction of the city*, where the noun *destruction* corresponds to the **main verb** of a clause, and *the city* to its **object**: '(Someone or something) destroyed the city'. The **subject** of the underlying clause can be expressed by a **genitive**, and **adverbs** can be represented by **adjectives**: *Hannibal's sudden arrival in the city = Hannibal suddenly arrived in the city*.

nominative   A traditional term for the **subjective** case. Compare **objective case**.

non-assertive   Lacking positive, affirmative meaning. **Questions** and negative statements tend to be non-assertive, in contrast to positive statements. This means that quantifiers such as *any*, *anyone, anything* (so-called ***any*-words**, tend to be used in them, in contrast to *some, someone, something,* etc. Compare:

> *I've watched **some** good games recently.* (assertive)
> *Have you watched **any** good games recently?* (non-assertive)
> *I haven't watched **any** good games recently.* (non-assertive)

The rule which replaces *some* etc. by *any* etc. is not absolute. There are, in fact, 'assertive questions' which contain words like *some*: *Have you watched **some** good games recently?* (These are 'loaded questions' expecting a positive reply.) Words like *any* can be termed non-assertive items. They include not only *any* and words beginning with *any-*, but also *ever, yet,* and *at all.*

non-assertive items   see **non-assertive**

non-count noun (also called **uncountable noun**)   A **noun** which has no **plural** use, and which cannot be used with 'counting' words such as *one, two, three, a few,* and *many.* Examples are **mass nouns** like *bread, milk, leather, steam, gold* which refer to substances and materials. But also many **abstract nouns** are non-count, e.g., *advice, health, music, sanity.* Non-count nouns contrast with **count nouns,** such as *street, table, child, meeting.* However, this contrast is over-simplified, since many nouns can be either count or non-count, according to meaning (compare *some paper* ~ *some papers, some change* ~ *some changes*). Also, nouns which are primarily non-count can be used as count nouns in special contexts. For example, *some sugar* (= mass substance) is normal, but *some sugars* could be used to mean either some lumps of sugar, or some types of sugar.

non-defining relative clause   see **restrictive and non-restrictive relative clauses**

non-finite   see **auxiliary verb**; **bare infinitive**; **-ing form**; **non-finite clause**; **participle**; **predication**; **verb phrase**

non-finite clause   A **clause** which has a non-finite verb phrase (see **non-finite verb** below). Non-finite clauses are subdivided into (a) infinitive clauses, (b) *-ing* **clauses**, and (c) *-ed* **clauses**. For example:

   (a)   *This is the best way* [*to serve dressed crab*].
   (b)   *They have an odd way of* [*serving dressed crab*].
   (c)   *The dressed crab* [*served in this restaurant*] *is excellent.*

Non-finite clauses are normally **subordinate clauses**. They are treated as clauses because thcy have elements such as **subject**, **verb**, and **object**. However, as in the examples above, although its meaning is implied, the subject of a non-finite clause is typically omitted. (See **finite clause**; **finite verb**.)

non-finite nominal clause   see **nominal clause**

non-finite verb   A **verb** form which is not finite, i.e. does not involve variation for **past** and **present tense**. The three non-finite verb forms are (a) the **infinitive**, with or without *to*, (b) the *-ing* **form** (often called present participle or gerund), and (c) the *-ed* (past participle) **form**:

   (a)   (*to*) *be*   (b)   *being*   (c)   *been*
         (*to*) *eat*   *eating*   *eaten*
         (*to*) *live*   *living*   *lived*

All verbs, except for **modal auxiliaries**, have non-finite forms.

Non-finite forms always follow the **finite verb** form (if any) in the **verb phrase**: *will be*, *is eating*, *has lived*, *has been living*, *will be eating*, etc. Such verb phrases are called finite, because they begin with the finite verb form. But, in addition, non-finite verb forms occur in non-finite verb phrases, which do not contain a finite verb. Types of non-finite verb phrases are (a) infinitive phrases (beginning with an infinitive form), (b) *-ing* phrases (beginning with an *-ing* form), and (c) *-ed* phrases (beginning with an *-ed* form). Examples of non-finite verb phrases are:

(a)	*to eat*	(b)	*eating*	(c)	*eaten*
	to be eating		*having eaten*		*seen*
	to have sent		*having been eaten*		*answered*

Modal auxiliaries like *can* are considered to be finite, because they come first in the verb phrase and have (at least to some extent) the present/past contrast of *can* ~ *could*, etc. (See **finite verb**.)

non-finite verb phrases   see **non-finite verb**; **perfect**

non-personal   An alternative term for **neuter**.

non-restrictive   Adding meaning to a **noun phrase** in a way which does not restrict or limit its reference. (See **restrictive and non-restrictive relative clauses**.)

notional concord   Concord (or agreement) where the choice of verb form is determined more by the meaning of the subject than its strict grammatical form. For example, with **collective nouns**, both of the following are acceptable:

*The audience **was** impressed by his performance.*
*The audience **were** impressed by his performance.*

The first sentence illustrates grammatical concord (singular verb with singular subject); the second (plural verb with singular subject) breaks grammatical concord, but observes notional concord. The notion of 'plurality' is present in the singular subject, since an audience can be easily thought of as consisting of a set of separate people. (See **Concord**.)

noun A very large class of words which refer to entities (persons, things, substances, places, and abstractions of various kinds). A noun can be the **head** of a **noun phrase**, and therefore the chief word in indicating the **subject** or **object** of a verb. Most **common nouns** have both a singular and a plural form, the regular **plural** being shown by the addition of -(*e*)*s* to the singular form: *boy ~ boys, cat ~ cats, church ~ churches, kindness ~ kindnesses,* etc. (There are also some **irregular plurals**, such as *woman ~ women, life ~ lives, sheep ~ sheep, formula ~ formulae.*) Nouns are subdivided into the following major categories: **common nouns** contrast with **proper nouns**; **count nouns** contrast with **non-count** (including **mass nouns**); **concrete nouns** contrast with **abstract nouns**; **collective nouns** contrast with **non-collective nouns**. Many words can be recognized as nouns by their suffixes, e.g., *-er* (in *reader*), *-or* (in *actor*), *-ess* (in *princess*), *-ness* (in *kindness*), *-ity* (in *sanity*), *-dom* (in *kingdom*), *-hood* (in *sainthood*), and *-ship* (in *friendship*). (See **noun phrase**.)

noun clause see **nominal clause**

noun phrase   A phrase which (typically) has a **noun** or a **pronoun** as its **head**, and which can have various functions in the sentence, notably that of **subject, object, complement,** or **prepositional complement.** (Certain kinds of noun phrases – especially time phrases like *last week* – can also be **adverbials.**) The structure of noun phrases can be stated as follows: (**determiner[s]**) + (**modifier[s]**) + **head** + (modifier[s]) where brackets represent optional elements. Often the phrase consists of a head alone – either a noun or a pronoun (e.g., *her, music, animals*): these could all be objects of a sentence beginning *I love* . . . The next most frequent type of noun phrase consists of a determiner (especially one of the **articles** *the* and *a/an*) with a following noun, as in *the music, an animal, those animals.* Before a singular **count noun**, there must be a determiner (e.g., *animal* without a determiner cannot be a noun phrase). To form more complex noun phrases, modifiers of various kinds may be added either before or after the noun head. One-word modifiers, especially adjectives and nouns, typically occur before the head: *a hungry child; folk music; these lively young animals.* On the other hand, multi-word modifiers, especially **prepositional phrases** and **relative clauses,** generally occur after the head: *the music of Beethoven; the music that I love best; the music of Beethoven that I love best.* Naturally, the modifiers which precede and which follow the head can be combined in one noun phrase, so that noun phrases of great length can be built up: *the recent unrest in Albania, which has led to a cautious measure of liberalization in a regime that up to recently has been a byword for totally inflexible authoritarianism.* As this example shows, noun phrases can become complex not only by combining different kinds of modifiers, but by the **embedding** of one phrase in another, and one clause in another. Noun phrases are so varied in their form that they allow some structures which are exceptions to the general rules given above. For example, multi-word modifiers can precede the head in the form of a genitive phrase: [*my mother's*] *bag*. Also, there are cases where the head of a noun phrase is an adjective: *the rich*, *the unemployed*, etc.

noun–pronoun concord   see **concord**

number   (1) The grammatical choice between singular (one) and plural (more than one). In English, **nouns, pronouns, determiners** and **present tense** verbs can vary for number: e.g., *student ~ students, I ~ we, that ~ those, takes ~ take*. (2) Another name for a numeral. (See **numerals**.)

numerals (also called **numbers**)   Words referring to number. The two main classes of numerals are **cardinal numerals** (*one, two, three, four* . . .) and ordinal numerals (*first, second, third, fourth* . . .). They may be written not only in letters, but in digits: *1, 2, 3, 4, . . . 15, . . . 66, . . . 1,000, . . .* or *1st, 2nd, 3rd, 4th, . . . 15th, . . . 66th . . .* and so on. Numerals have a small grammar of their own, within the larger grammar of the English language: for example, speakers of English know how to read aloud the numeral *11,362* (*eleven thousand three hundred and sixty-two*) even though they have probably not met with that particular number before. As for their grammatical function in sentence grammar, numerals behave rather like **determiners** and **pronouns**. Like determiners, they can precede the modifiers and head of a noun phrase: *three blind mice*; *our twenty-ninth wedding anniversary*. Like pronouns, they can also occupy the position of **head** of a **noun phrase**:

*What lovely cakes! I have eaten **three**.*
*Really? This is only my **second**.*

In addition, ordinal numbers can be used like **adverbs**, e.g., ***First**, let me introduce my family*; *In the final competition, Jason came **sixth***.

object   A part of a **clause** or **sentence** which normally follows the **main verb**, and corresponds to the **subject** of a **passive** clause or sentence. For example:

> $\Big\{$ *Armadillos eat **termites**.*   (*termites* is the object)
> *Termites are eaten by armadillos.*
> (*termites* is subject of the passive)

> *My best friend has bought **the house next door**.*
> *Charles is visiting **the Joneses** tomorrow.*

An object is usually a **noun phrase** (as in the examples above). If it is a **personal pronoun**, the **objective case** is needed: *me, him, her, us, them* – not *I, he, she, we, they*. An object can also be a **nominal clause**: *Everyone knows* [*that mercury is a metal*]; *People rarely believe* [*what she says*]. A useful way to identify an object is to consider it as an answer to a question with *What* or *Who(m)* + **auxiliary** + subject: *What do armadillos eat?*; *Who(m) is Charles visiting tomorrow?* In terms of meaning, the object is often identified with the person, thing, etc. that is affected by the action described by the verb. Whereas the subject typically represents the 'doer', the object typically represents the 'doee'. A clause may have an **indirect object**, in addition to a **direct object**: in *Charles is cooking **the family** a meal*, *the family* is the indirect object (representing those who are indirectly affected by the action) and *a meal* is the direct object. (See **complement**; **indirect object**; **passive**.)

object complement A **complement** which follows the **object**, and which describes some (putative) characteristic of what the object refers to. For example, in *Margaret has been keeping the house tidy*, *tidy* is the object complement, and *the house* is the object. The relation between the object and object complement is representable by the verb *be*: an implied meaning of the above sentence is that 'the house is tidy'. The object complement can be an **adjective (phrase)**, as above, or it can be a **noun phrase**, as in: *The empress declared Catherine her heir*. The set of verbs which permit an object complement is not large. In addition to *keep* and *declare* (illustrated above), it includes *leave, call, like, want, consider, find, think, get, make, send, turn, elect* and *vote*. Compare subject complement (see **complement**).

objective (case) The special form a **pronoun** takes when it has the role of **object** in a clause, e.g., *We admire her*. The objective forms of the **personal pronouns** are *me, him, her, us, them*, in contrast to the **subjective** forms *I, he, she, we, they*. (The *wh*-pronoun *who* also has an objective form *whom*, but increasingly *whom* is being discarded, even in object position, in favour of *who*.) The term 'objective' should not be taken to mean that these forms are found only in the object position: objective pronouns are also used following a **preposition**, and frequently in other positions (especially as **subject complement**), and after *than*, in which the subjective form is traditionally considered correct: *Hello! It's only me*; *You've won more games than us*. (See **case**.)

objective pronouns   see **objective**

omission   see **ellipsis; zero**

open and closed word classes   A major classification of **word-classes** (also called **parts of speech**). Open classes are those which have a very large membership, viz. **nouns, lexical verbs, adjectives, adverbs** and **numerals**. Closed classes, on the other hand, are those which have a rather small membership, viz. **conjunctions, determiners, interjections, operator**-verbs, **prepositions, pronouns**. The open classes are so called because it is easy to add new words to them by established processes of word-formation. For example: *tanorexia* (a new noun, meaning excessive anxiety about the colour of one's suntan); *unbundle* (a new verb); *eco-friendly* (a new adjective); *drop-dead* (a new adverb, used in the context 'drop-dead gorgeous') – (examples from *The Longman Register of New Words*, Vol. 2, 1990). In contrast, it is quite difficult to introduce (say) a new determiner or conjunction into the language. The distinction between open and closed classes is not absolute, and there is a scale of 'openness' in both categories: e.g., in the closed category, prepositions are relatively open. (See **lexical**.)

operator   A **verb** word which has a key role in forming **negative, interrogative**, and other types of 'derived' **clauses** or **sentences** in English. The class of operator verbs includes the **modal auxiliaries** *will, can, may, shall, must, would, could, might, should*; the finite forms of the auxiliaries *have* and *do*; and the finite forms of the verb *be* (both as an auxiliary and as a main verb). In addition, it includes the negative **contractions** of these verbs: *won't, can't,* *shan't, mustn't, wouldn't, mightn't, shouldn't, hasn't, haven't, hadn't, doesn't, don't, didn't, isn't, aren't, wasn't, weren't.* If we think of the 'basic' sentence pattern as that of a positive statement, such as *The dog has eaten its dinner*, then it is easy to form (a) negative, (b) interrogative, and (c) elliptical sentences by means of the operator as follows. (a) Place *not* after the operator, or replace the operator by its negative contraction: *The dog **has** not* (or ***hasn't***) *eaten its dinner.* (b) Place the operator in front of the **subject**: ***Has/Hasn't** the dog eaten its dinner?* (c) Delete whatever follows the operator: (*The cat hasn't eaten its dinner, but*) *the dog **has**.* An operator can be defined as either a finite auxiliary, or a **finite** form of the verb ***be***. It will be noted that some positive statements do not have an operator (viz. those with a finite **main verb** other than ***be***). In order for the operator rules (a)–(c) to work, these positive statements must be replaced by equivalent statements in which the dummy operator ***do*** is introduced:

> *It rained heavily last year.* ~
> (*It **did** rain heavily last year.*)*
> *It **didn't** rain heavily last year.*
> ***Did/Didn't** it rain heavily last year?*
> (*They said it would rain heavily last year, and*) *it **did**.*

The second sentence above, in parentheses and marked *, does not occur except when the operator is marked by strong emphasis. (See **auxiliary; ellipsis; emphasis; finite verb.**)

ordinal number/numeral   *see* **cardinal number/numeral; numerals**

participle   A traditional term for the non-finite *-ing* and *-ed* forms of the **verb**, especially when they are used in a quasi-adjectival way. Thus, in *They heard the children laughing* and *They heard the window being smashed/broken*, *laughing* and *being* are present participles, and *smashed* and *broken* are past participles. Compare **gerund**.

particle A useful term for a 'little word' which does not belong to one of the regular **word-classes**. For example, *not* can be called a 'negative particle'. In multi-word verbs like *make up*, *look after*, 'particle' is used for one of the words which follow the main verb, e.g. *up*, *after*. (See **phrasal verb**; **prepositional verb**.)

parts of speech A traditional term for **word-classes** (such as **noun**, **verb**, **adjective**, **preposition**).

passive, passive voice A type of verb construction in which a form of *be* is followed by the *-ed* **form** (past participle) of the **main verb**, e.g., *is loved, was beaten, will be sent*. By extension, a passive **clause** or **sentence** is one in which the **verb phrase** is passive. The effect of using the passive is to convert the noun phrase which would be the **object** of a corresponding non-passive (i.e. **active**) clause into the **subject**. For example:

> *A farmer **has found** the missing children.* (active)
> *The missing children **have been found** by a farmer.* (passive)

Thus the passive reverses the normal relation between the 'doer' and the 'done to'. The **agent** (the noun phrase following *by*) in the passive corresponds to the subject of the active clause. However, the agent is very frequently omitted: *The missing children have been found.* The passive is useful for various purposes. For example, if we want to place emphasis on the 'doer' as the most important piece of new information, the passive enables us to place the 'doer' after the verb, so giving it **end-focus**. On the other hand, if we want to omit information about the 'doer', we can simply omit the agent. Strictly, however, the agent does not have to be the 'doer' or performer of an action. Some verbs, such as *see*, are not action verbs, but can still be used in the passive: *The robbery was seen by several people.* In informal English, there is also a *get*-passive in which the first verb is *get*, instead of *be*: *The thief got caught by the police.*

past participle   A traditional term for the *-ed* participle form of verbs. (See *-ed* **form**; *-ed* **clause**.)

past participle construction   see *-ed* **clause**; **participle**

past perfect (traditionally called pluperfect)   A form of **verb phrase**, consisting of *had* + *-ed* **form**, in which the **perfect** construction is combined with the **past tense**, e.g., *had lived, had left, had written.* The meaning of the past perfect is: happening before a time in the past, i.e. 'past in the past': *When the party started, we were not aware that someone had stolen the birthday cake.* The past perfect can be combined with the **progressive** (e.g., *had been living*) or the passive (e.g., *had been eaten*).

past progressive   A form of the **verb phrase** in which the **past tense** is combined with the **progressive** construction: it consists of a past tense of *be* + *-ing* **form**, e.g., *was leaving, were helping.* Its meaning is that something was 'going on', i.e. in progress, at a definite time in the past: *Martha was staying at a hotel when she heard of her father's death.* The past progressive can be combined with the **passive**, e.g., *was being sold, were being taught.*

past simple (or simple past)   A form of the **verb phrase** in which there is just one **verb** – the **past tense** form of the **main verb**: *Joan enjoyed the concert.* The interrogative and negative equivalents of the past simple, except with (b), require the corresponding form of the dummy operator, *did/didn't*: e.g., *saw* ~ *Did . . . see?* ~ *didn't see.*

past tense   A form of the **verb** (e.g., *saw, looked, found*) which contrasts with the **present tense** (e.g., *see*[*s*], *look*[*s*], *find*[*s*]). The past tense indicates (a) that the happening took place at a definite time before the present, or (b) that the happening is seen as unreal, or hypothetical. For example:

(a) *Columbus discovered America in 1492.*   (past time)
(b) *If Columbus went to America today, he would be astonished.*
(unreal, hypothetical)

The regular past tense is formed by adding *-ed* (or *-d*) to the **base form** of the verb: *talk* ~ *talked, change* ~ *changed.* But there are over 200 **irregular verbs** (including **auxiliary verbs**) which form the past tense differently, e.g., *see* ~ *saw, take* ~ *took, meet* ~ *met. Be* is the only verb which has more than one past tense form: it has *was* (singular) and *were* (plural). A **verb phrase** can be made past by using the past tense of its first (**finite**) verb: *was eating, had eaten, was being eaten,* etc. Some **modal auxiliaries** do not have a past tense form, e.g., *must, ought to.* Historically, other modals do have past tense forms (*may* ~ *might, will* ~ *would*), but the past tense forms behave in some ways like independent verbs.

perfect (or perfective) **(aspect)**   A **verb** construction consisting of *have* + *-ed* **form**, e.g., *has happened, has lived, have eaten.* The perfect contrasts with non-perfect (e.g., **present simple** or **past simple** forms) and its meaning places the happening in a preceding time zone. The key idea of the perfect, therefore, is 'beforeness'. Contrast, for example:

> *She **works** in a factory.*   (at the present time)
> *She **has worked** in a factory.*   (at some time in the past)

The perfect combines with **modal auxiliaries**, e.g., *may have arrived, could have disappeared.* With *will*, it typically refers to a

FINITE:	PRESENT PERFECT	PAST PERFECT
Perfect simple	*has eaten* *has mended*	*had eaten* *had mended*
Perfect progressive	*has been eating* *has been mended*	*had been eating* *had been mended*
Perfect passive	*has been eaten* *has been mended*	*had been eaten* *had been mended*
NON-FINITE:	PERFECT TO-INFINITIVE	PERFECT -ING PHRASE
Perfect simple	*to have eaten* *to have mended*	*having eaten* *having mended*
Perfect progressive	*to have been eating* *to have been mending*	*having been eating* *having been mending*
Perfect passive	*to have been eaten* *to have been mended*	*having been eaten* *having been mended*

time seen in the past from a point in the future ('past in the future'): *By tomorrow, the snow will have disappeared.* The perfect can also combine with **progressive** (perfect progressive) and **passive** constructions, and occurs in non-finite verb phrases (perfect infinitive and -*ing* phrases). The table (p. 85) illustrates the main types of verb phrase in which the perfect occurs. (See **present perfect; past perfect.**)

perfect infinitive, perfect progressive   see **perfect**

person   A grammatical category which applies primarily to **pronouns**, and secondarily to **noun phrases** and **verbs**. **Personal pronouns** and **reflexive pronouns** are classified as first person (*I, we, ourselves,* etc.), second person (*you, yourself,* etc.) or third person (*she, he, it, they, herself,* etc.). First person pronouns refer to the speaker (or, in the plural, to the speaker and other people). Second person pronouns exclude the speaker, and refer to the hearer, with or without other people. The third person refers to people, things, etc. excluding both the speaker and the hearer. Apart from pronouns, person plays a role in the choice of the **finite verb**. The **-*s* form** of the verb (e.g., *takes, likes*) follows a third person singular **subject** (*he/she/it* **takes**), whereas the **base form** is used for first and second person singular, as well as all plural subjects (*I/you/they* **like**). Apart from personal pronouns, all other noun phrases are third person (*The cat* **likes**; *The cats* **like**). (See **personal pronouns; reflexive pronouns.**)

personal pronouns   The most important class of **pronouns**, referring to people, things, events, etc. which are understood to be known in the context. Personal pronouns frequently have an

antecedent, i.e. an expression to which they refer (or, strictly, co-refer) in the preceding or following context. For example, in *Carol tells me* **she** *is changing* **her** *job*, *she* and *her* most likely (though not inevitably) refer to Carol, who has been mentioned in the subject of the sentence. Personal pronouns vary on four dimensions: **number, person, case**, and **gender**, as shown in the table on p. 88. (See **case; gender; number; person; reflexive pronouns**.)

phrasal verb   A verb idiom which consists of two words, (a) a **main verb**, such as *take*, *find*, and (b) a **prepositional adverb** (often called a **particle**), such as *off*, *out*. Thus *take off*, *take out*, and *find out* are examples of phrasal verbs. Particularly in informal English, phrasal verbs are common and numerous. Their meaning is idiomatic: we cannot easily infer what the expression means from the meanings of its parts. Thus *take off* (in one of its senses) means 'imitate', and *find out* means 'discover'. Phrasal verbs can be (a) **intransitive** (i.e. not taking an **object**) or (b) **transitive** (i.e. taking an object):

(a) *As one aircraft* **took off**, *the other one was* **touching down**.
    (both verbs are intransitive)
(b) *I asked them to* **put off** *the meeting, but they decided to* **call** *it* **off** *completely*.   (both verbs are transitive,
    their objects being *the meeting* and *it*)

Notice that with transitive phrasal verbs, the position of the object varies. When the object is a **personal pronoun**, it comes before the particle (*call* ***it*** *off*). Otherwise, the object can occur either before or after the particle: *put* ***the meeting*** *off* or *put off* ***the meeting***. (See **phrasal-prepositional verb; prepositional verb**.)

Case →		SUBJECTIVE	OBJECTIVE	POSSESSIVE		
	Number ↓				1	2
1st	Singular	I	me		my	mine
	Plural	we	us		our	ours
2nd	Singular	you	you		your	yours
	Plural	you	you		your	yours
3rd	Singular	he, she, it	him, her, it		his, her, its	his, hers, its
	Plural	they	them		their	theirs
Person ↑	Gender →	m, f, n	m, f, n		m, f, n	m, f, n

Abbreviations: m = masculine, f = feminine, n = neuter

phrasal-prepositional verb A verb idiom which consists of three words, viz. **main verb** + **particle** + **preposition**. For example, *put up with*, *look forward to*, *do away with*. (See **phrasal verb**; **prepositional verb**.)

phrase A grammatical unit which may consist of one or more than one word, and which is one of the classes of constituent into which simple sentences can be divided. The main types of phrase are **noun phrase**, **verb phrase**, **prepositional phrase**, **adjective phrase**, and **adverb phrase**. Each is named after the **word-class** (**noun**, **verb**, etc.) which plays the most important part in its structure. (See **head**; **modifier**.)

place adverb/adverbial An **adverbial** (e.g., **adverb**, **prepositional phrase**, or **clause**) which answers the question 'Where?', 'Where to?', 'Where from?'. Examples include *here*, *to the meeting*, *wherever you want*.

pluperfect see **past perfect**

plural The form of a **noun, pronoun,** or **determiner** which indicates 'more than one', in contrast to the **singular**. For example:

	NOUN	PRONOUN	DETERMINER	(VERB)
Singular	*student*	*he/she/it*	*this/that*	*(comes)*
Plural	*students*	*they*	*these/those*	*(come)*

Verbs are included in the table because they choose plural when their **subject** is plural. The regular plural of nouns is formed by adding *-s*, *-es* to the singular form. There are also **irregular**

89

plurals: *man* ~ *men, wife* ~ *wives, mouse* ~ *mice, foot* ~ *feet, deer* ~ *deer, analysis* ~ *analyses.* Some irregular plurals coexist with alternative regular plurals: *people* or *persons, maxima* or *maximums, foci* or *focuses.*

positive   The opposite of negative; used, for example, of a clause or a sentence. (See **negation**.)

positive statement   see **operator; positive; statement**

possessive   An alternative term for **genitive.**

possessive pronouns   A set of **pronouns** which correspond in meaning and position to genitive nouns or **noun phrases**:

    (a) *my   your   his   her   its   our   their*
    (b) *mine   yours   his   hers   its   ours   theirs*

Their meaning can be one of 'possession' (e.g., **my** *garden* = 'the garden which belongs to me'), but they can also have other meanings associated with the genitive, as in **their** *arrival,* **our** *hopes.* The first possessive form – (a) above – occurs in the **determiner** position, preceding the noun and any modifiers (e.g., **their** *recent arrival at the hotel*). The second possessive form occurs in the position of a whole noun phrase, e.g., *My garden is tidier than* **yours** (= your garden). Like genitives, the second possessive pronoun can follow *of* in a 'double genitive' construction: *Jo is an old friend* **of mine**. **Personal pronouns** have possessive forms, and in addition *who* has the possessive form *whose*, and *one* the possessive form *one's*. (See **genitive; personal pronouns**.)

postdeterminer   A **determiner** which follows other determiners (especially central determiners like *the*, *this*, *my*) in the noun phrase. Examples of postdeterminers are *many* and *other* in *her **many** friends* and *the **other** day*.

postmodification   see **genitive**

postmodifier   A **modifier**, e.g., in a **noun phrase**, which follows rather than precedes the **head** of the phrase. Thus in *the President of France*, *of France* is the postmodifier of *President*.

predeterminer   A **determiner** which precedes other determiners in the **noun phrase**, including central determiners such as *the*, *this* and *my*. For example: *all*, *both*, and *half* in *all/both/half the schools* are predeterminers.

predicate   The part of a **clause** or simple sentence which follows the **subject**, and which consists of the **verb phrase** together with elements relating to it. For instance, in *The boat arrived on time*, *The boat* is the subject, and *arrived on time* the predicate.

predication   The part of a **clause** or simple sentence which follows the **subject** and **operator**, and which consists of the non-finite part of the **verb phrase**, plus other elements relating to it. When its content is known from the context, a predication can be omitted by **ellipsis**, or can be replaced by *do so*: *We have not yet sent you the order, but we will (**do so**) early next week.* (See **operator**; **predicate**.)

predicative adjective   An **adjective** which occurs in the position of **complement**, especially after the **verb *be***; e.g., *tall* in *My sister is* (*very*) *tall*. Some adjectives (e.g., *asleep*) are restricted to predicative use. Contrast **attributive adjective**.

premodifier   A **modifier**, e.g., in a **noun phrase**, which precedes rather than follows the **head**. For example, in a *Japanese custom*, *Japanese* is a premodifier of *custom*.

preposition   A word which typically comes in front of a **noun phrase**, e.g., *of, in, with* in *of milk*, *in the building*, *with all the good intentions I had at the beginning of the year*. The noun phrase which follows the preposition is known as a **prepositional complement**, and the preposition together with its complement is known as a **prepositional phrase**. The prepositional complement may also be a **nominal clause** (e.g., *for [what we are about to receive]*). In some circumstances, prepositions do not have a following prepositional complement, and they are then referred to as **Stranded Prepositions**, e.g., at the end of many **wh-questions** and **relative clauses**, where the 'fronted' **wh-word** or **relative pronoun** has the role of prepositional complement: *What is this machine for? I'll ask the man that I was talking to*. Prepositions include some very common words, such as *at, on, by, over, through, to*. In addition, there are quite a few **complex prepositions** which are written as more than one word: *away from*; *instead of*; *in front of*; *by means of*, etc. The meanings of prepositions are very varied, but two important categories are those of place and time relations: *at the airport*, *in the summer*, etc.

prepositional adverb   An **adverb** which is identical (or similar) in form to a **preposition** to which it is also related in meaning, e.g., *on, by, off, over, about, past*. (Words like *out* and *away* can be considered prepositional adverbs, because of their relation to the complex prepositions *out of* and *away from*.) Prepositional adverbs, unlike their matching prepositions, do not have a **prepositional complement**. For example, in *He jumped over the fence*, *over* is a preposition, but in *He jumped over*, it is a prepositional adverb. Similar examples are: *She fell down the stairs* and *She fell down*.

prepositional complement The grammatical element (typically a noun phrase or pronoun) which follows a preposition. (See **noun phrase; preposition; prepositional adverb; *wh*-clause**.)

prepositional object see **prepositional verb**

prepositional phrase A **phrase** consisting of a **preposition** (e.g., *to*) followed by a **noun phrase** (or **nominal clause**), e.g., *to my best friend*. Prepositional phrases have two main functions in grammar. (a) They can act as **postmodifiers** in a noun phrase (e.g., *the kindest member of my family*). (b) They can also act as **adverbials**, specifying, for example, the time or place of an action described in the rest of the clause: *The train will start its journey at midnight. It will leave from platform four*. (See **preposition**.)

prepositional verb A verb idiom consisting of a **main verb** followed by a **preposition**, e.g., *look after*, *look at*, *decide on*, *consist of*, *cope with*. The choice of preposition is determined by the verb, rather than by the independent meaning of the preposition. Prepositional verbs can be confused with transitive **phrasal verbs**, but they are clearly distinct in that the **particle** (or second word) of a prepositional verb is a preposition, whereas that of a phrasal verb is a **prepositional adverb**. The confusion arises because of the similar appearance of examples like:

> *I looked **at** the picture.* (*at* = preposition)
> *I looked **up** the word.* (*up* = prepositional adverb)

But the difference is clear when we note that *the word* can be moved in front of its particle (*I looked the word up*), whereas *the picture* cannot: **I looked the picture at* is ungrammatical.

The **noun phrase** following a prepositional verb is called a prepositional object. Its role in the sentence is similar to that of the **object** of a **transitive verb** (compare, for example, *I looked at the picture* with *I examined the picture*).

present continuous   An alternative term for **present progressive**.

present participle   The *-ing* **form** of the **verb**, especially when used in a quasi-adjectival way, e.g., *standing* in *the man standing by the door*. (See **gerund; participle; past participle**.)

present perfect (or present perfective)   A **verb** construction which combines the **present tense** with the **perfect aspect**, consisting of *has/have* + *-ed* **form** (e.g., *has received, have gone*). The present perfect refers to something taking place in a period leading up to the present moment:

> (a) *I **have lived** in Kent since I was a baby.*

The present perfect therefore competes with the **past tense** in referring to past time. But note that in (a), *have lived* indicates a past state of affairs continuing up to the present, while the **past simple** (e.g., *was, lived*) indicates a state of affairs which existed at a definite time in the past, and which no longer exists now. Thus, the present perfect is distinguished from the past simple as referring to the 'past with relevance to the present'. This 'present relevance' may be either a matter of continuation up to the present, or alternatively an implication that the effects of an event in the past continue to the present time:

    (b) *My brother **has won** £1,000.*   ('He has the money now')

    (c) *Mary **has injured** her arm.*   ('Her arm is still bad')

Compare the past simple *Mary **injured** her arm (last week), but it's better now.* In some contexts, however, the past tense and the present perfect are both acceptable, and the meaning difference between them is not always significant.

present perfect progressive A verb construction which combines the **present tense** with the **perfect** and **progressive** constructions: *has/have been* + *-ing* **form** (e.g., *have been waiting*). This combines the idea of 'past with present relevance' with the idea of 'going on over a (limited) period': *I'm tired – I've **been working** all day.*

present perfective see **present perfect**

present progressive (also called present continuous) A verb construction combining the **present tense** with the **progressive**, and consisting of *am/is/are* + *-ing* **form** (e.g., *is reading, are playing*). The present progressive, rather than the **present simple**, is used to describe events or activities going on at the present time. *It's **raining** heavily outside; The home team **are playing** brilliantly this afternoon.* The present progressive can also be used to refer to planned future happenings: *I'm **playing** golf with Sandy tomor-*

row. Note, however, that verbs referring to states (e.g., *be*, *know*, *seem*, *resemble*) do not go easily with the progressive. We use these verbs with the present simple to describe an ongoing state: *Terry **seems** tired this evening* (not: **is seeming*). (See **present simple; progressive (aspect)**.)

present simple (or simple present)   A form of **verb phrase** in which there is just one verb: a **present tense** form of the **main verb** (e.g., *looks* in *This house **looks** old*; or *look* in *These houses **look** old*). The present simple is the most widely used form of verb phrase in English. It is used for a range of meanings with reference to present time, and is even used occasionally for past and future events. But note that the **present progressive** takes up some of the 'semantic space' which the present simple has in other languages, being used for temporary happenings in progress or in prospect at the present time. Contrast, for example:

> *We **give** him money for his birthdays.*
> (a general statement, implying that this is an annual habit)
> *We **are giving** him money for his birthday.*
> (a specific statement, about what is happening this year only)

The **interrogative** and **negative** equivalents of the present simple (except with the verb *be*) require the use of *does/do* as a dummy operator. (See **operator; present tense**.)

present tense   A form of the **finite verb** which contrasts with the **past tense**, and consists of either the **base form** (e.g., *give*) or the *-s* **form** (e.g., *gives*) of the verb. The *-s* form is used for the third person singular; in all other circumstances the base form is used. The present tense generally indicates that what the verb describes takes place in a span of time including the present – but there are exceptions to this, such as the **historic present** (referring to the past).

primary verbs The three **verbs** *be*, *have*, and *do*, which are the three most common and important verbs in English. The primary verbs function both as **auxiliary verbs** and as **main verbs**.

pro-form A substitute form; i.e. a word or expression which has no detailed meaning of its own, but has the function of 'standing in the place' of another (often more complex) expression. **Personal pronouns** are the most familiar examples of pro-forms. Other examples are the pronoun *one* (e.g. in *this one*, *a new one*), and the verbal forms *do* and *do so* (substituting for a **predicate** or a **predication**).

progressive (aspect) (also called **continuous**) A **verb** construction consisting of *be* + *-ing* **form**, e.g., *is watching*, *were smoking*, *be walking*, *been writing*, in contrast to non-progressive forms like *watches*, *smoked*, *walk*, and *written*. In meaning, the progressive indicates an event or activity in progress over a limited period. It also has implications of incompleteness: *I have washed the car* definitely implies that the job is finished, while *I have been washing the car* does not. (See **aspect**; **past progressive**; **present progressive**; **verb phrase**.)

pronouns A class of words which fill the position of **nouns** or **noun phrases**, and which substitute for, or cross-refer to, other expressions. The most important class of pronouns is that of **personal pronouns**, which vary for **person** (*I*, *you*, *she*), **case** (*I*, *me*, *my*), **number** (*I*, *we*) and **gender** (*he*, *she*). Other classes are **reflexive pronouns** (e.g., *myself*), **interrogative** pronouns (e.g., *what*), **relative pronouns** (e.g., *which*), **demonstrative pronouns** (e.g., *this*) and **indefinite pronouns** (e.g., *someone*). Pronouns function as the **heads** of noun phrases, and in fact usually constitute the whole of a noun phrase, since **modifiers** occur with them rather rarely. (Examples of modified pronouns are *poor little **me**, **you** yourself, **what** on earth, **those** who live abroad, **someone** else*.)

proper noun   A **noun** which is spelt with an initial capital letter, and which refers to an individual (e.g., an individual person, or an individual place). Proper nouns contrast with **common nouns**, which denote classes of entity (e.g., *boy* denotes the class of immature male human beings). Proper nouns do not normally have **articles** or other **determiners** (e.g., *Thomas* is normal, *the Thomas is not). Further, they do not vary for **number**: most proper nouns (e.g., *Eliza, Kennedy, Athens, Jupiter*) are singular, and a few (e.g., names of mountain ranges such as *the Rockies*) are plural. In exceptional cases, names like *Kennedy* change their number and occur with articles (e.g., *the three Kennedys*); but in these cases the proper noun (*Kennedy*) has been converted into a common noun, referring to a set of people with the name (*Kennedy*). (See **naming expressions**.)

purpose adverb/adverbial   An **adverb(ial)** which adds information about the purpose or aim of an action: *in order that, so that, in order to, so as to*, and *to* (+ **infinitive**) are all ways of introducing an **adverbial clause** of purpose. Purpose adverbials answer the question 'Why?': *Why did the Johnsons leave early? (They left early) **to catch the last bus**.*

regular verbs

question A type of **sentence** or **clause** which has an 'information gap' (e.g., in *When did you post the letters?* the information gap is the time at which the stated event occurred). Therefore a question is typically interpreted as requesting information from another person. (But there are also questions – e.g., **rhetorical questions** – which do not have this function.) Direct questions end with a question mark (*?*). The major types of question are *yes–no* **questions**, *wh*-**questions**, and **alternative questions**. (See also **echo question; rhetorical question; tag question**.)

question words see **intensification; interrogative;** *wh*-**word**

reflexive pronouns A class of **pronouns** closely related to **personal pronouns** and ending in *-self/-selves*. They are: *myself, yourself, himself, herself, itself, ourselves, yourselves, themselves, oneself.* Reflexive pronouns typically occur later than the **subject** and **verb** in a clause or sentence, and are identical in reference to the subject: *Jacob injured **himself** playing football*; *I am not **myself** today*; *Many authors write novels about **themselves***. In an **imperative** sentence, *yourself* (singular) or *yourselves* (plural) can be used: *Please make **yourselves** comfortable*. A second use of reflexive pronouns is for **emphasis**: *She **herself** cooked the dinner* means 'She, and no one else, cooked the dinner'. The emphatic reflexive pronoun is placed in **apposition** to another **noun phrase** – in this case, the subject *She* – but may be separated from it for **end-focus**: *She cooked the dinner herself.*

regular plural see **plural** (Contrast **irregular plurals**)

regular verbs see **verb** (Contrast **irregular verbs**)

relative adverb *When* and *where* at the beginning of a relative clause: *the moment **when** the bomb exploded*; *the place **where** I was born*.

relative clause A **clause** which normally acts as a **modifier** in a **noun phrase**, and which gives information about the **head** of the noun phrase (or **antecedent**): *I talked to the people [who live there]; The computer [which they bought] was very powerful*. In these examples, *(the) people* and *(the) computer* are antecedents; *who* and *which* are **relative pronouns**, i.e. the words which refer back to the antecedent, linking the relative clause to it. The relative pronouns in English are *who/whom/whose, which, that*, and **zero**. A zero relative pronoun is the missing element (marked below by [ ]) which occurs at the beginning of a relative clause where *that, which* or *whom* could occur:

> (a) *I'll comment on some of the points* [[ ] *you raised*].
>   (= **which** *you raised*)
> (b) *The people* [[ ] *she works with*] *are very friendly*.
>   (= **whom** *she works with*)

The relative pronoun has varied functions in the relative clause. For example, in *which you raised* (a), *which* is the object; in *whom she works with* (b), *whom* is a prepositional complement. The term relative clause is also applied to clauses introduced by a **relative adverb**. Moreover, by extension, it is applied to clauses which contain a relative pronoun, but which have a whole clause or sentence as their antecedent: so-called **sentential relative clauses**, e.g., *He treats his wife like a doormat, **which annoys me**. (See also **restrictive and non-restrictive relative clauses**.)

relative pronoun   A **pronoun** which introduces a **relative clause**, and which links it to the **antecedent**, or **head** of the **noun phrase** of which it is a part. The English relative pronouns are *who/whom/ whose* (normally referring to people), *which* (referring to things), *that* (mainly referring to things), and **zero** (see **relative clause** above). *Who* is a **subjective** form, *whom* an **objective** form, and *whose* a **possessive** form. (The zero relative pronoun is like an objective form – it cannot be used as **subject**.) The use of *whom*, however, is no longer common, and in **informal** English, *that*, zero, or *who* is used instead: compare *the woman to whom we were talking* with the more informal *the woman we were talking to*. (See **relative clause**; *wh*-**word**.)

reported command   see **reported speech**

reported question   see **reported speech**

reported speech (or indirect speech)   The language we use to report what someone else said, using our own words. Thus if Mary said '*I am sorry for John*', someone could report this as: *Mary said that she was sorry for John*. This is called a reported statement, because the original speech was in **statement** form. Reported speech is distinguished from **direct speech**, in which the original speech is repeated in the original words, normally enclosed in quotation marks. There are also reported questions. For example, if Mary said '*What did you say?*', this could be reported by the hearer as *Mary asked me what I had said*. And there are reported commands, requests or suggestions. Thus, if Mary said '*Please sit down*' to Alan, this could be reported: *Mary told/asked Alan to sit down*. The following are useful 'ground rules' for reported speech:

(a) It is normal to put reported speech in a **subordinate clause**:
 (i) If the original speech was a statement, use a *that*-clause:
 . . . *that she was sorry for John.*
 (ii) If the original speech was a **question**, use a *wh*-interrogative clause: . . . *what I had said.*
 (iii) If the original speech was a command/request/suggestion, use a *to*-infinitive clause: . . . *to sit down.*
(b) If the original contained a **present tense**, change it to a **past tense**: . . . *was sorry for John.*
(c) Where the original contained a past tense, use a **past perfect**: . . . *what I **had** said.*
(d) Where the original contained a **personal pronoun**, change its **person** to the person appropriate to the situation in which it is being reported; typically this will mean changing first- and second-person pronouns to the third person: *that **she** was sorry for John.*

Basically, these ground rules say: 'When you report speech, use the forms appropriate to *your* situation, rather than the original speech situation'. They are not to be applied as mechanical rules, because of many exceptional circumstances which cannot be described here.

reported statement   see **reported speech**

response form   A word whose special function is in responding to the speech of another speaker. In English, *Yes* and *No* are the chief **positive** and negative response forms.

restrictive and non-restrictive relative clauses   A major classification of **relative clauses** (also called defining and non-defining relative clauses). Restrictive relative clauses are so called because they *restrict* the reference of the **noun phrase** they belong to. For instance, in

*Most families **who own their own homes** support the government's housing policy.*

who own their own homes is restrictive, specifying *which* or *what kind of* families. But if we insert commas before and after the relative clause, it becomes non-restrictive:

*Most families, **who own their own homes**, support the government's housing policy.*

This sentence now makes two separate statements: (a) that most families support the government's policy, and (b) that most families own their own houses. Non-restrictive clauses do not restrict the reference of the noun phrase, but add an independent piece of information about it. A non-restrictive clause has to have a **wh-word** (usually *who* or *which*) as its **relative pronoun**. It cannot have *that* or a zero relative pronoun. (See **relative clause; relative pronoun.**)

result adverbial   An **adverbial** specifying the result or outcome of the happening described in the rest of the **clause**. Result adverbials can be clauses introduced by *so that*, or *to*-infinitive clauses: *All the doors were locked, **so that they had to climb in through a window**; I woke up **to find the house deserted**.*

rhetorical question   A **question** which does not seek information, but rather implies that the answer is self-evident. *Who can say* *what will happen?* has the effect of a forceful statement: *No one can say what will happen.*

-s form   The form of the **verb** which ends in *-s* or *-es*, e.g., *makes, wishes, adds.* The *-s* form is used when the **subject** of the verb is third person singular (see **person**): *She writes*; *He forgets*; *Time passes.* The verbs *be* and *have* have the irregular *-s* forms *is* and *has.* (The *-s/-es* ending is also used for the regular **plural** of **nouns**.) (See **concord**; **number**; **plural**.)

second person   see **person**; **reported speech**

second-person pronoun   A **pronoun** which refers to the hearer/ reader (with or without other people, but excluding the speaker/ writer). The English second-person pronoun is *you, your, yours, yourself, yourselves.* As a **personal pronoun**, it has the same form (*you*) for singular and plural, **subjective** and **objective**.

sentence   The unit of language which it is the business of grammar to describe. In writing, sentences are marked by beginning with a capital letter and ending with a full stop (.), question mark (*?*), or exclamation mark (*!*). In spoken language, the definition of a sentence is more problematic. There are no 'watertight' definitions of the sentence, but it is useful to think of it as the largest unit of grammar, at the head of a hierarchy of grammatical units:

A sentence consists of one or more clauses.
A **clause** consists of one or more phrases.
A **phrase** consists of one or more words.
A **word** consists of one or more morphemes.
   (Morphemes = stems or affixes.)

Sentences may be divided into simple sentences (those which consist of just one clause) and **complex** or **compound sentences** – those which contain more than one clause. If we restrict our attention to the simple sentence (e.g., *My brother plays tennis every weekend*), then we can talk about dividing the sentence into **subject** (*My brother*) and **predicate** (*plays tennis every weekend*), or into elements such as subject, **verb phrase** (*plays*), **object** (*tennis*) and **adverbial** (*every weekend*). But strictly, these are components of the clause rather than of the sentence. The first stage of analysing a sentence, then, is to recognize whether it has a single **main clause**, as above, or more than one main clause, as in:

(*Today's weather will be fine*), *but* (*tomorrow will be cloudy and wet*).

(See **complex sentence; compound sentence; sentence types**.)

sentence adverb or **sentence adverbial**   An **adverb** or **adverbial** which is peripheral to the **clause** or **sentence** it belongs to, and qualifies the whole of the rest of the clause or sentence, e.g., *As you know* in *As you know, I'm leaving my present job*; or *frankly* in *The play was disappointing, frankly*. Sentence adverbials are divided into **conjuncts** and disjuncts. Conjuncts are **linking adverbials** which have a sentence-connecting function, such as *moreover*. Disjuncts are adverbials which imply the attitude of the speaker to the form or content of the rest of the clause/sentence, such as *as you know* and *frankly* above.

sentence (or sentential) **relative clause**   A **relative clause** which refers back to the whole of the preceding clause or sentence. In *Elaine keeps mice in her bedroom*, [*which is eccentric, to say the least*], the part in parentheses is a sentence relative clause.

sentence types Sentences can be classified into major types according to their meaning and function in discourse. The four types which are traditionally recognized, in order of importance, are **statements, questions**, commands (i.e. **imperative** sentences) and **exclamations**. A single **compound sentence** can sometimes include more than one of these types. The following combines a command and a statement: *Leave the building immediately, or I'll summon the police.*

sentential relative clause see **sentence relative clause**

simple past see **past simple**

simple present see **present simple**

simple sentence see **predication; sentence; subject**

singular see **number; plural**

specific definite and indefinite articles see **generic**

statement The proposition expressed by a simple sentence in the declarative form (i.e. in which **subject** is followed by **predicate**), e.g., *Her secretary works upstairs.* Here *Her secretary* is the subject, and *works upstairs* is the predicate. A statement can be negated (*Her secretary doesn't work upstairs*). Also, a statement can be either true or false, and is typically used to convey information; in these respects it contrasts with **questions**, commands, and **exclamations**. It can be argued, however, that statements do not have to be expressed in a declarative form: e.g., a

rhetorical question, such as *Am I my brother's keeper?* has the force of a statement in **interrogative** form. (See **reported speech; sentence types**.)

stranded preposition   see **preposition**

subject   The element of a **clause** or simple sentence which normally comes before the **verb phrase** and consists of a **noun phrase**. Thus, in *These cars are expensive* and *Recently they have raised taxes*, *these cars* and *they* are the subjects, preceding the verb phrases *are* and *have raised*. The subject of a clause may also be a **subordinate clause**: [*That he confessed to the crime*] *proves nothing*. Subjects can be recognized by a number of additional factors: (a) they have **concord** with the **finite verb**; (b) they are placed after the **operator** in **questions**: *Are these cars expensive?*; *Have they raised taxes?*; (c) they typically refer to the 'doer' of an action. This last factor, however, is unreliable: e.g., in **passive** clauses, the subject does not refer to the 'doer', a role usually taken by the **agent** (if present) instead: *Taxes have been raised by the government*.

subject complement   see **complement**

subjective (case) (also called **nominative**)   The form taken by a **personal pronoun** when it acts as **subject** of a **clause** or **sentence**. The subjective pronouns are *I, he, she, we, they*. The pronouns *you* and *it* are both subjective and **objective**. *Who* is a subjective **interrogative** and **relative pronoun**, but it is also widely used in objective functions. (See **case; objective (case)**.)

subject–verb concord   see **concord**

subjunctive (**mood**)   A form of a **finite verb** sometimes used to express non-factual or hypothetical meaning. The subjunctive was formerly much more common than it is today. It survives only in three rather formal contexts. (a) The mandative subjunctive, in *that*-clauses such as *This committee will urge that the president resign his office.* (b) The formulaic subjunctive, as in *God bless* you! *Good fortune be yours!* (c) The *were*-subjunctive, as in *If I were you, I would accept the offer.* In (a) and (b), the subjunctive is the **base form** of the verb, and contrasts with the **-s form** which is normal after a singular subject. In (c), *were* is used instead of the expected form *was* after a singular subject, to express unreal or hypothetical meaning.

subordinate clause   A **clause** which is part of another clause, termed the **main clause**. Subordinate clauses are classified according to their position or function in the main clause.

(a) **Nominal clauses** take on functions associated with **noun phrases**, e.g., **subject** or **object** in the main clause.
(b) **Adverbial clauses** take the function of **adverbials**.
(c) **Relative clauses** take an 'adjectival' function, as **modifiers** in a noun phrase.
(d) **Comparative clauses** take a modifying function in an **adjective phrase**, an **adverb phrase**, or a noun phrase, following a **comparative** word or construction.

subordinating conjunction   see **conjunction**

subordination   A method of linking or relating two clauses by making one clause subordinate to another. Contrast **coordination**. (See **subordinate clause**.)

substitute form, substitution   see **pro-form**

superlative   The form of a **gradable word** which ends in *-est* (or *-st*), e.g., *oldest, longest, most, least*. The superlative denotes the highest or lowest position on some scale of quality or quantity, e.g., *Mount Everest is the **highest** mountain in the world*. One-syllable gradable **adjectives** and **adverbs** form their superlative by adding *-est*, but for most adjectives and adverbs of more than one syllable it is necessary to add the preceding adverb *most* (or *least* for the opposite end of the scale), e.g., *most useful, most quickly, least important*. There are a few irregular superlative forms, such as the adjectives/adverbs *best, worst* and the pronouns/determiners/adverbs *most, least*. (See **comparative; gradable words**.)

syntax   The part of grammar which analyses the way **words** are combined into **sentences**. It contrasts with **morphology** (the grammar of word-structure). In English, most of grammar is concerned with syntax, because morphology is relatively simple.

tag question   A short **question** which is added after a **statement**, to elicit a confirming response from one's hearer, e.g., *... aren't you?, ... isn't she?, ... were they?* English has a broad range of tag questions, whose choice depends on the grammatical form of the statement. The rules for forming the most common types of tag questions are:

(a) Copy the **operator** of the statement, and change it to negative if positive, or to positive if negative:

> *Jo **is** late, **isn't** she?*
>
> *You **haven't** seen my glasses, **have** you?*

(b) If there is no operator, use the positive or negative form of the '**dummy** auxiliary' *do:*

> *She **likes** sugar in her coffee, **doesn't** she?*
>
> *The photos **came** out well, **didn't** they?*

(c) If the subject of the statement is a **personal pronoun**, copy it and place it after the operator in the tag question:

> *We've met before, haven't **we**?*

(d) If the subject of the statement is not a personal pronoun, replace it in the tag question by the personal pronoun which matches its referent (in **number**, **person**, **case**, and **gender**):

> *The **journey** will not take long, will **it**?*

tense The grammatical contrast between **present** and **past** forms of the **finite verb**: *look(s)* ∼ *looked, take(s)* ∼ *took*. (See **past tense; present tense**.)

***that*-clause** A **subordinate clause** which begins optionally with the conjunction *that*, and fills **nominal** positions, such as **object** (a), **complement** (b) or **subject** (c), in the sentence:

(a) *He told me* [***that his mother was ill***].

(b) *Our hope is* [***that the situation will improve***].

(c) [***That opinions will differ***] *is inevitable.*

Note that in object position (a), the *that* can be omitted: *He told me his mother was ill. That*-clauses normally have the force of a **statement**, e.g., in **reported speech**. They can occur (with or without *that*) as a prepositional complement, but the preposition preceding them is omitted: in *I'm afraid (that) you will miss the train*, the *of* that would follow *afraid* in other constructions is omitted before *that. That*-clauses often occur as postponed subjects after **introductory** *it*: instead of (c), it is more usual to say, *It is inevitable that opinions will differ.* (See **extraposition.**)

third person see **person; personal pronouns; present tense; reported speech**

time adverb/adverbial An **adverb(ial)** which adds information about the time of the happening described by the rest of the clause, e.g., *now, recently, on Monday, since I saw you last.* The commonest type of time adverbial answers the question 'When?'. Two other types of time adverbial are those of **frequency** (answering the question 'How often?') and of **duration** (answering the question 'How long?'):

> *Last Saturday, the match had to be cancelled.*   (time–when)
> *The phone bill has to be paid every month.*   (frequency)
> *Why don't you stay with us for a week or two?*   (duration)

time conjunction see **adverbial clause**

to-infinitive The form of the **verb phrase** which begins with *to* + the **infinitive (base form)** of a verb. As the following examples show, the *to*-infinitive can be combined with the **perfect, progressive,** and **passive** constructions:

to-infinitive

> to go   to have taken   to be dying
> to be seen   to have been eating to have been caught

To-infinitive verbs are used to introduce *to*-infinitive clauses, which are a common class of **non-finite clauses**. The *to*-infinitive clause usually has no **subject**, although its subject is implied by the context. It may, however, have **objects**, **complements**, and/or **adverbials**. Some of the variety of structures of *to*-infinitive clauses is illustrated by:

(a) *to resign*   (verb phrase alone)
(b) *to start | the motor*   (verb phrase + object)
(c) *to have been beaten | by the champion*   (verb phrase + *by* +agent)
(d) *to become | a doctor*   (verb phrase + complement)

To-infinitive clauses can have varied functions in the sentence; they can be:

(a) **nominal clauses** (e.g., as subject – including postponed subject in **extraposition** – or object of the main clause:

> **To have been beaten by the champion** *is no disgrace.*
> *It is no disgrace* **to have been beaten by the champion.**
> *I have been wanting* **to resign** *for years.*

(b) **adverbial clauses** (especially as adverbials of **purpose**):

> **To become a doctor**, *you need to pass a lot of exams.*

(c) **adjectival clauses** (i.e. similar to **relative clauses**):

> *This is the way* **to start the motor**.

The subject of a *to*-infinitive can be expressed, if necessary, by using *for* + **noun phrase**:

(112)

transitive verb

It is no disgrace for a novice to be beaten by a champion.
What would be the best way for us to contact you?

Compare **bare infinitive**.

to-infinitive clause see **infinitive**; **non-finite clause**; **reported speech**; **result adverbial**; **to-infinitive**

transferred negation The placement of the **negative word** *not/n't* in a **main clause**, whereas logically speaking it belongs to a **subordinate clause**: *I don't suppose that Jill remembered the tickets.* Here the *not* appears to negate the supposing, rather than the remembering. But in fact, we understand the sentence to express a supposition that Jill didn't remember the tickets. Another construction favouring transferred negation is *seem/appear* followed by a *to*-infinitive: *He didn't seem to notice* is equivalent to *He seemed not to notice.*

transitive verb A main verb which requires an object to complete its meaning. For example, the verb *make* is transitive, since the object cannot be omitted in sentences such as: *This factory makes excellent furniture.* (**This factory makes* doesn't make sense.) If no **object** or **complement** follows, as in *The first attempt failed*, the verb is termed **intransitive**. A transitive verb can normally be used in the **passive**: *Excellent furniture is made by this factory.* However, many verbs are transitive in one context and intransitive in another. Examples are *open* and *finish*.

TRANSITIVE USE	INTRANSITIVE USE
Someone opened the door.	*The door opened.*
They have finished the game.	*The game has finished.*

(We can add **adverbials** optionally after these verbs: *Someone opened the door suddenly*; *The game has finished already*. But this does not affect their classification as transitive or intransitive.)

uncountable noun   see **non-count noun**

universal conditional clause   A **clause** which begins with a word like *whoever*, *whatever*, *whichever*, *whenever*, or *however*, and which has an **adverbial**, **conditional** role in the sentence: *However old you are, you should take plenty of exercise*. The meaning is: 'It doesn't matter how old you are', etc. (See **wh-ever word**.)

verb   A large class of words which indicate events and states of affairs, or which help qualify the reference of other verbs. Verbs are divided into two main classes: the class of **main verbs**, which has a very large membership (e.g., *appear*, *drop*, *end*, *understand*, *revivify*) and the class of **auxiliary verbs**, which has a small membership of important verbs (*be*, *have*, *do*, *will*, *can*, *may*, *shall*, *would*, *could*, *might*, *should*, and *must*). Of the auxiliary verbs, *be*, *have*, and *do* are known as primary verbs – they can also act as main verbs. The remaining auxiliary verbs are known as **modal auxiliaries**. Except for cases of **ellipsis** (e.g., *I will* said in answer to a question *Will you have this man to be your husband?*), almost every clause or simple sentence has a main verb. One or more auxiliary verbs can be added before the main verb, helping to specify its manner of reference, e.g., to specify time, **aspect**, or modality. Apart from modal auxiliaries, all verbs have a variety of forms. Most verbs are regular verbs and have four forms, e.g., *help*, *helps*, *helped*, *helping*. **Irregular verbs** (of which there are over 200) include many common verbs, and all auxiliary verbs.

verb pattern

The number of forms they have varies from one (the modal auxiliary *must*) to eight (the most common verb of all, *be*). The functions these forms perform in the verb phrase divide into those of **finite** and **non-finite verbs,** as this table shows:

FINITE				NON-FINITE		
Present tense		**Past tense**	**Imperative/ Subjunctive**	**Infinitive**	***-ing* participle**	**Past participle**
Base form	*-s* form	*-ed* form	Base form	Base form	*-ing* form	*-ed* form
look *see*	*looks* *sees*	*looked* *saw*	*look* *see*	(*to*) *look* (*to*) *see*	*looking* *seeing*	*looked* *seen*

The table shows, first, the forms of a regular verb, *look*, and, second, the forms of an irregular verb, *see*. As a regular verb, *look* has the *-ed* **form** *looked* for both the past tense and the past (*-ed*) participle. But, like many irregular verbs, *see* has a distinct past participle form ending in -(*e*)*n*. (See **finite verb; irregular verbs; non-finite verb; verb phrase.**)

verb complementation   see **verb pattern**

verb construction   see **construction; passive, passive voice; verb phrase**

verb pattern   (also called clause pattern) A pattern which contains a **main verb** and whatever elements have to follow that verb to complete its meaning grammatically. For example, the commonest verb pattern in English is that of a **transitive verb,** which has to be followed by a **direct object:**

SUBJECT (S) | VERB (V) | OBJECT (O)
The council | has *built* | *a new office block.*

Note that *The council has built* is incomplete: something else is required, both grammatically and semantically, viz. an object. The element(s) required after the verb is/are called the complementation of the verb. Using the symbols S (= **subject**), V (= **verb phrase**), O (= **object**), C (= **complement**) and A (= **adverbial**) for the elements of clause structure, we can represent a number of verb patterns as follows:

SV   *Jonathan's pet hamster | has **died**.*   **(intransitive verb)**

SVO   *The chef | is **preparing** | something special.*   **(transitive verb)**

SVC   *Everyone | was **feeling** | hungry.*   **(linking verb)**

SVA   *Your travel agent | is | on the phone.*
       (pattern with obligatory **adverbial**)

SVOO   *We | should have **wished** | them | a happy New Year.*
       (pattern with **indirect object**)

SVOC   *Meg's behaviour | is **driving** | her parents | mad.*
       (pattern with **object complement**)

Each pattern specifies what is required for completeness: but optional adverbials can always be added. For instance: *The chef is preparing something special **this evening***. There are many more patterns than these, some of them requiring **subordinate clause** structures as part of the complementation. They include:

I | imagined | that Jane was lonely.   V + ***that*-clause**

I | imagined | her | to be happy.   V + O + ***to*-infinitive** clause

I | imagined | meeting her in the street.   V + ***-ing* clause**

From these examples, it is also clear that the same verb can take a number of different verb patterns. (See **phrasal verb**; **prepositional verb**.)

verb phrase   1 A phrase consisting of one or more **verb** words. The verb phrase is the most essential and pivotal element of a clause. It consists of a **main verb** alone (a simple verb phrase), or a main verb preceded by one or more **auxiliaries**. (There is also an elliptical verb phrase which consists of an auxiliary verb with **ellipsis** of the main verb.) The verb phrase involves five principal choices. The first choice, of **tense**, is between present and past tense, and involves choosing the appropriate form of the **finite verb**, e.g., *am/is/are* ∼ *was/were*; *has/have* ∼ *had*; *write(s)* ∼ *wrote*. The remaining four choices are whether to use two-verb constructions, whether alone or in combination. They are:

MODAL CONSTRUCTION
modal auxiliary + infinitive   *must eat*
PERFECT CONSTRUCTION
have + past participle   *has eaten*
PROGRESSIVE CONSTRUCTION
be + *-ing* participle   *is eating*
PASSIVE CONSTRUCTION
be + past participle   *is eaten*

These constructions can be combined in the order stated:

MODAL + PERFECT
modal auxiliary + *have* + past participle   *must have eaten*
MODAL + PROGRESSIVE
modal auxiliary + *be* + *-ing*   *must be eating*
MODAL + PASSIVE
modal auxiliary + *be* + past participle   *must be eaten*
PERFECT + PROGRESSIVE
have + *been* + past participle   *has been eating*

PERFECT + PASSIVE
have + *been* + past participle   *has been eaten*
PROGRESSIVE + PASSIVE
be + *-ing* + past participle   *is being eaten*

And a further combination, viz. of three constructions, is also possible though rare:

MODAL + PERFECT + PROGRESSIVE
modal auxiliary + *have* + *been* + *-ing*   *must have been eating*
MODAL + PERFECT + PASSIVE
modal auxiliary + *have* + *been* + past participle   *must have been eaten*
MODAL + PROGRESSIVE + PASSIVE
modal auxiliary + *be* + *being* + past participle   *must be being eaten*
PERFECT + PROGRESSIVE + PASSIVE
have + *been* + *being* + past participle   *has been being eaten*

Verb phrases can be either finite or non-finite. In finite verb phrases, the first or only verb is a **finite verb**, and following verbs, if any, are non-finite. In non-finite verb phrases (e.g., *eaten, to eat, having been eaten*) all the verbs, both auxiliaries and main verb, are non-finite. 2 In some versions of grammar, the verb phrase is defined as a bigger unit, including not only the verb constructions above, but also the elements of a clause which follow the main verb, such as its object (see **predicate**). (See **passive; perfect; progressive; verb; verb pattern.**)

verbless clause/construction   A grammatical unit which resembles a **clause**, except that it lacks a **verb phrase**. Verbless clauses are often clauses from which the verb *be* has been omitted by

ellipsis: *A large crowd of refugees, **many of them women and children**, were imprisoned in the football stadium.*

verbless sentence   see **exclamation**

vocative   A **noun phrase** (often a single **noun**) loosely adjoined to a sentence, identifying the person or people addressed: *Oh, Thérèse, I'd like to have a word with you*; *Well done, **you boys**.* Vocatives behave like **sentence adverbials**, in that they can occur at the beginning or end of a sentence, or even in the middle, as in: *Come in, **Mr Wibley**, and make yourself at home.*

voice   The grammatical category which involves the choice between **active** and **passive** forms of the **verb phrase**. (See **passive (voice)**.)

***were*-subjunctive**   see **subjunctive**

wh*-clause**   A **subordinate clause** which begins with a ***wh*-word** or ***wh*-element**. There are two major kinds of *wh*-clause: (a) *wh*- **interrogative** clauses, and (b) *wh*-**relative clauses**, including **nominal relative clauses**. A *wh*-clause beginning with the conjunction *whether* is a subordinate ***yes–no* question**, e.g., in **reported speech**: *The visitors asked/wondered [**whether** there was any mail for them]*. A *wh*-clause beginning with other *wh*-words/phrases can be a subordinate ***wh*-question**: *I inquired [**what time** they served dinner]*. An important aspect of *wh*-clauses is that they require the *wh*-element to be placed at the beginning of the clause, even if this means changing the normal order of **subject, verb, object,** etc. Thus it is common for a *wh*-clause to have the order object, subject, verb, . . ., where the *wh*-element is the object: *I don't care **what you say. In other cases the *wh*-element may be a **prepositional complement** (a), a subject complement (b), or an **adverbial** (c):

> (a) *It's a problem [**which** we all have to live with]*.
> (b) *No one could guess [**how old** he was]*.
> (c) *It's a mystery [**where** those birds go in winter]*.

When the *wh*-word is (the first word of) a prepositional complement, there is a choice between a **formal** and **informal** construction. The formal construction places the **preposition** at the beginning of the clause, whereas the informal construction leaves it 'stranded' at the end – compare (a) with the formal equivalent: *It is a problem [**with which** we all have to live]*. When the *wh*-element is subject of the clause, no change in the normal statement order is needed: *I can't remember [who lives there]*.

***wh*-element**   A **phrase** consisting of or containing a ***wh*-word**. *Wh*-elements normally begin with a ***wh*-word** (e.g., *who, which chair, how often, whose car*), but one exception to this is the formal construction of a prepositional phrase in which the *wh*-word is preceded by a **preposition**, e.g., *in which, for how long*. (See ***wh*-clause**.)

***wh-ever* word**   A member of a class of words which resemble ***wh*-words**, from which they are derived by the addition of the suffix *-ever*: *whoever, whichever, whatever, wherever, whenever, however*, etc. *Wh-ever* words begin **nominal relative clauses** and **universal conditional clauses**.

***wh*-interrogative clause** see **nominal clause; reported speech; *wh*-clause**

***wh*-question** A **question** which begins with a ***wh*-element**: *Where are you? Who can we get to help us? How long have you been waiting here? Under what conditions have the prisoners been released?* As these examples show, *wh*-questions typically require a change of the normal statement word order: (a) the *wh*-element is placed at the beginning, even if it is object, complement, etc., and (b) there is **inversion** of the **subject** and the **operator** (e.g., *we can ~ can we*). There is no change of word order, however, when the subject itself is the *wh*-element: ***Who** said that?* (See **interrogative; question**.)

***wh*-word** A member of a small class of words which are **pro-forms**, filling a position at the front of a **question, exclamation**, or ***wh*-clause**, e.g., an **interrogative** or **relative clause**. Placing *wh*-words in initial position usually entails displacing them from their normal position in the sentence. The *wh*-words are: *who, whom, whose* (pronouns); *which, what* (pronouns and determiners); *how, when, where, why* (adverbs). The ***wh-ever* words** *whoever, whichever, wherever*, etc. behave in a similar way.

word A basic grammatical unit which also largely corresponds to the main unit of the dictionary. In writing, words are marked as the smallest units to be separated by spaces. However, there is no 'watertight' definition of a word: many **compounds**, for example, are on the boundary of what makes a single word, as opposed to a **phrase**. One useful criterion for words (as distinct from smaller units, such as roots and suffixes) is their relative independence in being inserted, omitted, or moved around in the sentence. (See **morphology**; **syntax**; **word-class**.)

word-class (traditional term: **parts of speech**) A set of words which form a class in terms of their similar form, function, and meaning. (That is, a word-class is a meeting point of **morphology**, **syntax** and semantics.) The word-classes which have a (very) large membership are **nouns**, **lexical** verbs, **adjectives**, **numerals** and **adverbs**. The word-classes which have quite a small membership are **operator**-verbs, **determiners**, **pronouns**, **prepositions**, **conjunctions** and **interjections**. (See **open and closed word-classes**.)

word-order A term which is often used rather loosely to refer to the order in which elements occur in a clause or sentence. Within **phrases**, the ordering of words in English is relatively fixed: we have to say *a very old car*, rather than **an old very car*, **car old very a*, etc. Within **clauses**, the ordering of phrases as **subject**, **verb**, **object**, **adverbial**, etc. is more flexible, particularly regarding the position of adverbials. Nevertheless, English is often termed a relatively 'fixed word-order language', because, compared with many other languages (and subject to some well-known exceptions), the order of elements such as subject, verb and object is relatively inflexible. (See **end-focus**; **end-weight**.)

yes–no question A common type of **question** which invites the hearer to choose between two possible answers, *yes* or *no*. A *yes–no* question is closely related to a **statement**: in fact, it can be described as a question as to the truth or falsehood of a statement. It is usually distinguished from a statement (a) by **word-order**, and (b) by a rising intonation pattern, in speech. To form a *yes–no* question, place the **operator** (i.e. the first auxiliary or main verb *be*) in front of the subject:

STATEMENT	YES–NO QUESTION
subject + operator . . .	operator + subject . . .
You could wash the dishes.	*Could you wash the dishes?*
The clock has been mended.	*Has the clock been mended?*
The children are in bed.	*Are the children in bed?*

If the statement contains a simple verb phrase without an operator, the *yes–no* question must contain the appropriate form of the '**dummy** auxiliary' *do* + the **base form** of the **main verb**:

Sheila enjoyed the party.   Did Sheila enjoy the party?

Yes–no questions can also be **negative**: *Couldn't you wash the dishes?*; *Hasn't the clock been mended?* These are 'loaded questions', expressing surprise that the answer to the question is apparently negative. Another kind of loaded question is a *yes–no* question which keeps the statement order, and relies on intonation to indicate its interrogative force: *You enjoyed the party?* This is a 'just checking' question, and expects a positive answer.

zero article   An **article** which is omitted before a **common noun**. The zero article is the normal way of expressing indefinite meaning before (a) a **non-count noun**, or (b) before a **plural count noun**, e.g., *water, trees*. The zero article contrasts with the **definite article** *the* (used for definite meaning in front of all common nouns) and the **indefinite article** *a* or *an* (used for indefinite meaning in front of singular count nouns).

zero item   A word or suffix which is omitted, and which leaves vacant a structural position in a phrase or clause. Examples of this omission are **zero articles**, zero relative pronouns, and zero *that* (in ***that*-clauses** without an introductory *that*). (Compare **ellipsis**.)

zero plural   An irregular plural of a noun, where the plural form is identical to the singular, e.g., *sheep*, *deer*, *series*, *aircraft*.

zero relative clause   see **cleft sentence; relative clause**

zero relative pronoun   see **relative clause; relative pronoun**